Reviving Indigenous Water Management Practices in Morocco

This book demonstrates how Morocco and other semi-arid countries can find solutions to water scarcity by rediscovering traditional methods of water resource management.

The book begins by examining indigenous water heritage, considering the contribution of Islam and the mixed influences of Greek and Roman, Middle Eastern, Andalusian, and Berber cultures. It then provides a thorough examination of resource management practices in Morocco throughout history, tracing the changing patterns from the instillation of agrarian capitalism in the XIXst c., through the Protectorate years (1912–1956), to the XXIst c. The book explains how reviving and modernizing traditional methods of water management could provide simple, accessible, and successful methods for addressing XXIst c. challenges, such as water scarcity and climate change. The work concludes by highlighting how these indigenous practices might be used to provide real-world practical solutions for improving water governance and therefore developing sustainable water management practices.

Reviving Indigenous Water Management Practices in Morocco will be of great interest to students and scholars interested in water resource management, indigenous peoples, traditional knowledge, and sustainable development.

Sandrine Simon holds a PhD in Ecological Economics from Keele University, UK. She has worked as a Research Fellow for Forum for the Future, lectured at the Open University, UK, at the Centre for Complexity and Change, and at the Euro-Mediterranean University of Fès Morocco (UEMF). She is currently based as a researcher at the Interdisciplinary Research Centre for Education and Development (CeiED) of the Lusofona University of Lisbon, Portugal, where she focuses on urban agriculture, resilient cities, and territorial education.

Earthscan Studies in Water Resource Management

Water, Creativity and Meaning
Multidisciplinary Understandings of Human-Water Relationships
Edited by Liz Roberts and Katherine Phillips

Water, Climate Change and the Boomerang Effect
Unintentional Consequences for Resource Insecurity
Edited by Larry Swatuk and Lars Wirkus

Legal Rights for Rivers
Competition, Collaboration and Water Governance
Erin O'Donnell

Water Allocation Law in New Zealand
Lessons from Australia
Jagdeepkaur Singh-Ladhar

Reciprocity and China's Transboundary Waters
The Law of International Watercourses
David J. Devlaeminck

Water Management in China's Power Sector
Xiawei Liao and Jim W. Hall

Reviving Indigenous Water Management Practices in Morocco
Alternative Pathways to Sustainable Development
Sandrine Simon

Reviving Indigenous Water Management Practices in Morocco

Alternative Pathways to Sustainable Development

Sandrine Simon

Routledge
Taylor & Francis Group

LONDON AND NEW YORK

First published 2021
by Routledge
2 Park Square, Milton Park, Abingdon, Oxon OX14 4RN

and by Routledge
605 Third Avenue, New York, NY 10158

Routledge is an imprint of the Taylor & Francis Group, an informa business

© 2021 Sandrine Simon

British Library Cataloguing-in-Publication Data
A catalogue record for this book is available from the British Library

Library of Congress Cataloging-in-Publication Data
Names: Simon, Sandrine, 1970– author.
Title: Reviving indigenous water management practices in Morocco: alternative pathways to sustainable development / Sandrine Simon.
Other titles: Earthscan studies in water resource management.
Description: Abingdon, Oxon; New York, NY: Routledge, 2021. |
Series: Earthscan studies in water resource management |
Includes bibliographical references and index.
Subjects: LCSH: Water-supply–Morocco–Management. |
Water resources development–Morocco. |
Traditional ecological knowledge–Morocco. |
Sustainable development–Morocco.
Classification: LCC HD1699.M8 S56 2021 (print) |
LCC HD1699.M8 (ebook) | DDC 333.9100964–dc23
LC record available at https://lccn.loc.gov/2020054009
LC ebook record available at https://lccn.loc.gov/2020054010

ISBN: 978-0-367-61109-5 (hbk)
ISBN: 978-0-367-61113-2 (pbk)
ISBN: 978-1-003-10417-9 (ebk)

Typeset in Times New Roman
by Newgen Publishing UK

To my father, re-rooted in 'Berber-land'. In honour of Amazigh-Free men's lessons in resilience.

Contents

Preface

The urge to write this book stemmed from two important premises.

First, despite Morocco being water-independent (it does not share its surface nor underground water with any of its neighbouring countries), and although some of its regions are water-rich, water stress has dramatically increased in the last few years. Whether they emerged from water management practices based on too greedy (thirsty) demands, or whether they resulted from climate change, these water shortages now constitute a hard constraint that needs to be dealt with. Identifying best appropriate solutions to manage water has become a priority that will have consequences in all dimensions of the "development" of the country.

Secondly, current world-scale shocks, such as the Covid-19 pandemic, have encouraged people to question the ways in which we have recently managed our societies. Alternative schools of thoughts such as Ecological Economics[1] or Complex Adaptive Management[2] are not seen as being so controversial after all, and bringing them together could help us to analyse better the human–ecological interactions that must be better understood if we wish to manage our natural resources and habitat in a better, more resilient, and long-term basis. Above all, it is our societies and their culture underpin the ways in which we decide to manage these interactions.

This book is organized into three parts.

The objective of the first one is to explore this human–nature relationship by focusing on indigenous communities approaches. In the context of Morocco, we are interested in observing how the Berbers' ways of living were (still are?) supported by specific water management practices which, throughout centuries, constituted a rich water and agricultural heritage. By observing how various civilisations (Roman, Greek, Nabatean, Arab) contributed to this heritage throughout time, the two chapters explain how an agro-ecological-based type of livelihood developed that is resilient, adaptable to various natural environments, but also relevant at all times.

Despite the fact that indigenous know-how could contribute to a better understanding of what sustainable water management means, the Berber movement has struggled, not so much in asserting itself but, above all, in ensuring that Berber, rural know-how, needs, and opinions would better be taken into account in strategic decision-making.

Understanding why such participatory governance is so weak can be done by critically exploring how modern water management systems and, in particular, modern water governance systems, came to be. This is what Part II of the book concentrates on, through a historical perspective that explores the transformations in land management that occurred, from the XIXth c., throughout the Protectorate period, and then in the post-independence era. This evolution in three steps built the pillars of modern water management, based on market-economy principles, that have been in conflict with traditional water management. Intensive, industrial, irrigated agriculture turned towards exports. Private-public partnerships, the new reliance on technology and the focus on large-scale infrastructure, as well as changes in water laws and water stakeholders ..., All this deeply disturbed the society. These modern approaches followed a top-down approach and marginalized the rural world. The ecological and social outcomes of these preferred strategies have resulted in creating new constraints that cannot be ignored, and that call for alternative approaches to development.

Reinventing the way in which water management is being envisaged – its priority, the interactions it encourages between actors, the links it maintains between economic and ecosystem functioning – is what Part III focuses on. In a first chapter, it explains how climate change constraints led to adaptation strategies and how these encouraged critical thinking on what "development" now means, in a "post-modern" world. The second chapter then explores the notion of appropriate technologies and, through a set of illustrative examples, examines how traditional water management systems could potentially be adapted to the current context and respond to current (and future) constraints and needs. Finally, the third chapter points to one of the trickiest change factor. By looking at land management and the recent project of advanced regionalization and decentralization, it demonstrates why reforming water governance is so difficult and slow and why integrating indigenous know-how in strategic policy-making may still have a long way to go.

Despite obstacles on the ground, changes in water management are on their way and integrating indigenous know-how and needs into them is not impossible. A worldwide phenomenon can currently be observed that calls for alternative modes of development and finds in indigenous practices some important ecological–economic lessons that would help societies become more resilient and adaptive. Far from being old-fashioned concepts, these are precisely what strong, forward-looking, societies will have to be based on.

Notes

1 **Ecological Economics** is a school of thoughts that emerged in the 60s, encouraged by publications such as Silent Spring (written in 1962 by Rachel Carson). One of its main objectives is to question the validity of economics as a discipline being currently very close to "chrematistics" (in Greek: the "art of creating money"), when it should instead follow the Greek principles of "oikonomia" (the type of management of resources that meets the needs of the household). Assimilating the household to human communities, EE works on the principles following which economics is about understanding better the interactions between humans and the natural environment upon which they depend, in view of creating better welfare and resilience over the long-term. Authors such as Martinez-Alier, Daily, Meadows, Proops and O'Connor defend this approach.

2 **Complex Adaptive Management** is an approach originally based on eco-logical principles that explains the resilience of ecological species to shocks. The various stages of adaptation described by Holling have been seen as insightful when trying to understand how human communities could become more resilient and how the way in which they use natural resources could be more closely related to how ecological species function. Based on the premise that human communities and ecological systems are closely linked, this school of thoughts fundamentally questions the parameters (e.g. time scales, indicators of "success") used in current economic paradigms. It also highlights the importance of learning to work with uncertainty.

Part I

Indigenous North African water heritage

A lesson in agro-ecology

Introduction

As Healy et al. (2013) have shown, a need for more participatory research that would involve citizens on the ground and promote social learning between decision-makers and practitioners was expressed at the end of the XXth c. Efforts were undertaken to improve collaborative decision-making processes (EU 7th Framework Research "Science and Society Programme" 2008–2011) that would encompass a full spectrum of approaches, frameworks, and methods, from interdisciplinary collaboration through stakeholders negotiation to transdisciplinary deliberation and citizen participation. This movement stem from the needs felt by numerous communities to democratize decision-making and policy, reinvent public governance piece by piece from the bottom-up, and improve livelihoods.

One important part of this movement came from decision-makers themselves, who realized that, when it came to operationalizing sustainable development, they both had to involve people more in the decision-making process but also could benefit from learning from local knowledge, closer to environmental resources and milieu.

Another growing part of this movement has been identified as "the environmentalism of the poor and the indigenous" (Martinez-Alier, 2002). This has generated interest on indigenous practices and has also highlighted some important shortcomings in current development policies. What is for sure is that "indigenous culture" has its place in developmental issues and that it could contribute to designing alternatives to communities' survival and resilience if carefully studied, rediscovered, and integrated in forward-looking policies.

Optimistically, El Faiz (2015) stressed that:

> people around the world have become more conscious of the relevance of indigenous knowledge and know-how, and of the ability of traditional practices to improve agriculture and the rural world. Only a few example suffice to illustrate the role that the arabo-muslim agronomic hydraulic experience has had in the development of agricultural practices and in ensuring, for centuries, a sustainable and equitable management of arid and semi-arid ecosystems.
>
> (p. 230)

Thanks to the rediscovery of these traditional practices, research had been carried out by agronomists in Tunisia (Salaheddine El Amami) and in Morocco (Paul Pascon), as well as by architects (Pietro Laureano), in order to restore ancient techniques that could contribute to improving water management (El Faiz, 2015). Their efforts resulted in the creation of the UNESCO Chair of traditional know-how. As El Faiz highlights, one wonders why, therefore, years later, these water traditional engineering systems haven't been funded and used as development leverage systems. In the current context, they might become priority targets in research institutes that are focused on operationalizing sustainable development.

In Morocco, Berber people of various origins constitute the "indigenous community". Originally nomadic people, they progressively settled in rural environments, mostly in mountainous areas. Throughout history, they have developed agricultural and water management techniques that are well-adapted to particularly harsh climatic and sociopolitical conditions. Inhabitants of the country of Morocco as we know it today, they were both people of the land and some of the greatest dynasties. However, the colonization of the country by the French, followed by its independence and, more importantly, the pan-Arabism movement, put Arab culture at the forefront, at the expense of Berber culture. Despite Berbers' will to be recognized as Moroccans, their culture was progressively hidden behind the supremacy of the Arab Muslim one and the non-Berber Alawi dynasty.

Recently, a Berber movement has emerged. This has occurred at a time when *"across the globe, 'culture' as a category is being upheld as a right, an object of political struggle, and a commodity to be marketed"* (Maddy Weitzman, 2015: 2501). A series of campaigns has focused on making Moroccans rediscover various aspects of Berber (or "Amazigh") culture. For instance, as Gagliardi stressed:

Moroccan women, and especially Amazigh female figures, suffered most from the pan-Arabist, elitist and male construction of national identity. (…) Amazigh militants have promulgated a redefinition of Morocco on the basis of its pre-colonial and pre-Islamic Berber heritage, and have sought political change to preserve Berber culture and language as a "human right".

(2019: 3)

Throughout the start of the XXIst c., indigenous peoples' representatives have been extremely active. Due to their efforts, there have been some notable achievements. For instance, the Indigenous Peoples' Major Group on Sustainable Development Goals (SDGs) and the International Indigenous peoples Forum on Climate Change had a voice at the 21th Conference of Parties (COP21) of the UN Framework Convention on Climate Change (UNFCCC), held in Paris in December 2016 (Vinding and Mikkelsen, 2016).

However, despite the energy carried by the Berber Movement and King Mohamed VIth's willingness to value the Amazigh culture, "*there is no constitutional recognition of ancestral lands, group or indigenous rights*" (Gagliardi, 2019: 7). Besides, Morocco is not a state party to the ILO Indigenous and Tribal People Convention 1989 (no. 169) and was absent during the voting on the United Nations Declaration on the Rights of Indigenous Peoples (UNDRIP). This is not entirely surprising considering that, in 1930, the Berber Dahir (decree) enacted during the Protectorate, had been aimed at dividing Berbers from Arabs through the enforcement of separate judicial systems (Gagliardi, 2019: 7). Although defending Amazighity was then directly linked to the *current* reluctance of the Moroccan state in valuing Berber culture, know-how and land use, is more complex. As Oluborode Jegede (2016) stresses, this can be explained by the fact that land use policies in post-independence African states have been informed by a modern market-oriented development model which had no regard for indigenous peoples' concept of land tenure and use. Therefore, as Vinding and Mikkelsen (2016: 13) conclude, "*the root cause of many indigenous peoples' socio-economic poverty is their precarious situation when it comes to land and resource rights*". Focusing on the marginalization and impoverishment of the rural, largely Berber population, must be part of the Berber movement's demands. Integrating Berber culture in Moroccan developmental debates and strategy should therefore go well beyond a "folkloric add-on" and aim at making people learn from indigenous approaches to environmental protection through land management.

Supporting social–ecological systems whose stewards have had to continuously adapt and innovate implies protecting the rights of local and indigenous peoples to maintain their ways of life. In Morocco, indigenous communities living in and with the rural world could greatly contribute to tackling climate change pressure by providing insights into adaptation methods and resilience. However, although they have recently gained official recognition, their cultural heritage and know-how must be further explored and understood if it is to be taken seriously and integrated in the developmental strategies of the country.

Part I explores who indigenous communities of Morocco are, how a set of traditional water management systems have been developed throughout time within Berber communities, and what place defending traditional water management practices really has, in the context of the Berber revival movement.

References

El Faiz, M. (2015) *Agronomie et agronomes d'Al Andalous (XI –XIVe s.)*. Casablanca: La croisée des chemins.

Gagliardi, S. (2019) Indigenous peoples' rights in Morocco: subaltern narratives by Amazigh women. *The International Journal of Human Rights*. 23 (1): 281–296.

Healy, H. et al. (Eds) (2013) *Ecological Economics from the Ground Up*. London: Earthscan.

Maddy-Weitzman, B. (2015) A turning point? The Arab Spring and the Amazigh movement. *Ethnic and Racial Studies*. 38 (14): 2499–2515.

Martinez Alier, J. (2002) *The Environmentalism of the Poor; A Study of Ecological Conflicts and Valuation*. Cheltenham: Edward Edgar.

Oluborode Jegede, A. (2016) *The Climate Change Regulatory Framework and Indigenous Peoples' Lands in Africa: Human Rights Implications*. Pretoria, PULP.

Vinding, D. and C. Mikkelseon (2016) *The Indigenous World 2016*. Copenhagen: IWGIA.

1 Reviving indigenous water heritage

The indigenous communities of North Africa

The first inhabitants

The geographical location of Morocco, door to so many different environments and civilizations, evokes passageways of communities and memorable episodes in the history of the relationships between the Northern and Southern shores of the Mediterranean Basin. As historian Tourabi stressed:

> At the very cultural roots of what used to be called "Al Maghrib Al Aqsa" (the far west), stood some of the main characters of the Greek mythology. It is [there] that the giant Atlas lived and gave his name to the channel of mountains shaped in a North-East – South-West crescent that Zeus condemned him to carry on his shoulders. There also that Hercules created the Strait of Gibraltar by breaking a mountain with his swords, hence splitting definitively Europe from Africa.
>
> (2012: 2)

The first inhabitants of Morocco seem to have been called the "pebble people", from the tools that were found in archaeological sites close to Casablanca. They lived there between about 125,000 and 75,000 BC, when warm temperate and semi-tropical woodland covered much of North Western Africa. Then, came the last Ice Age, when "modern humans" spread around the Mediterranean from south East Asia. Around 12,000 BC, the *Oranian* culture emerged in what is now known as Western Algeria and spread into what is now known as Morocco. The wetter climate started to end in 5000 BC and, by the IIIrd millennium BC, the final stages set in. As the Sahara expanded, it split the

Maghreb off from sub-Saharan Africa and anchored it more firmly in the Mediterranean basin. The climatic conditions that developed in Morocco by the end of the Ist Millenium BC were roughly those that exist today, although the landscape has changed over the last 2000 years (Pennell, 2009: 4).

Contemporary to the Greeks, the Phoenicians, coming from what is now known as Lebanon, ventured towards the West of the Mediterranean Basin. Great sailors, they had little interest in invading inland territories but transformed the Mediterranean as one of the greatest trading sea, scattering their marks by creating trading ports after the VIIIth c. BC. These included Rusaddir (now Melilla), Tamuda, near Tetouan, Ksar es-Seghir and Tingis (Tangier). The greatest of all, founded around the end of the IXth c. BC, was Carthage, in what is now known as Tunisia. Later, they even ventured further down the coast of Africa where, from the town now known as Essaouira, they traded one of the most valuable commodities in the ancient world: purple dye (Pennell, 2009).

Berber communities first appeared in Africa 9000 years ago (Tourabi, 2012: 2) and became the "stabilised communities inhabiting this region". Amongst them, Pennel (2009: 7) listed the *Mauri*, a tribal federation of pastoral communities who based themselves in the West from the IVth c. BC, the *Masaeslyi*, a century later, whose kingdom stretched from the Moulouya river to Constantine in Algeria, and the *Massyli*, nearer Carthage. These communities had spread over the "grand Maghreb" after taking power in Egypt in 950 BC and creating a dynasty ruled by Chechonq the 1st – the start of which also corresponds to the beginning of their calendar (Tourabi, 2012).

The Roman province of Tigitana and the birth of the Berber *name*

Progressively, various kingdoms and dynasties, most of the time made up of confederations of tribes, were created. Whilst the Phoenician language was used for diplomatic and administrative purposes, the Berber language was used as an exchange language. When the Romans, expanding their already vast empire, invaded North Africa in the IVth c., the Phoenician power collapsed and the Berber communities – whom the Phoenicians used to call the Moors, "the Western populations" – started asserting themselves, notably by creating alliances with the Romans. Doing so allowed them to expand their territories. Nevertheless, Caesar abolished all the native kingdoms and only kept that of Bocchus, the only one to have supported him (Pennel, 2009: 11). That kingdom, allied with the Romans, reigned for three centuries and functioned as a federation of Berber tribes with a centralized monarchy. Caesar was murdered in 44 BC and Bocchus died in 33 BC. From

25 BC, Juba II presided over the Romanization of the North-West of Africa from what is now known as Algeria. Volubilis, the second city of his kingdom, developed into a great metropolis. Although he was a faithful ally of Rome, his son, Ptolemy, could not control the tribes and was murdered. This marked the end of the Berber kingdoms and, from then on, North Africa was ruled by Roman administration.

As Pennel (2009) noticed, the Roman province of Mauritania Tingitana was never as rich a province as Afriqyia (modern Tunisia). Besides, the Roman occupation of that province was *"never a matter of all-conquest: the Romans confined themselves to cities that were themselves largely autonomous"* (p. 14). The products of the extensive agriculture developed in the Volubilis area (where around a hundred olive presses were found, with indication of wine production as well as fishing on the Atlantic coast) were mostly exported. Historians showed that relations between Romans and Berbers were not always peaceful. In fact, as a result of pressure from unsubmitted tribes in the southern frontier, Volubilis was abandoned by its Roman administrators in 285 who, instead, preferred remaining in control only in Tangier (Tingis) and Salé (Pennell, 2009: 15).

Pennel (2009: 2) and Tourabi (2012: 4) explain that it is Ibn Khaldun, famous historian of the XIVth c., who popularized the term "Berbers" to design the people of Northern Africa. The term Berber is a Graeco-Roman expression that associates the name Berber to its Latin origin "barbarians". The Roman invaders could not understand the language of the people living in these territories, outside the Roman Empire and "foreign" to the Greek language and culture. Although Berber populations mixed with the Romans, and most certainly learned some agricultural techniques and how to build water infrastructure (sewage systems were put in place in Roman Volubilis and the Romans had built aqueducts to bring clean water to the city), animosity was kept all along. The *Berbers* really did remain the communities that were different, not understood, not understandable, and towards whom no curiosity was shown.

Admittedly, these were confusing times and the "indigenous communities" were being invaded, attacked, influenced, and merged with various and varied communities, cultures, and religions. Were the "Berber culture and practices" easily identifiable or, instead, still in the process of asserting themselves? Whilst Romans were in place and starting to fight Christianity in the East, Christianity was spreading within Morocco, even in the abandoned interior where Romans had not ventured. Some, amongst Berber, mostly polytheist, communities, started converting to Christianism. Most had been in contact with Jewish communities and culture for centuries. As Howe stresses, *"while the Phoenicians eventually disappeared, the Jews stayed, becoming part of the North African identity until the exodus to Israel in the mid XXth c."* (2005: 58). In the IVth c., the Vandals, a Germanic people on the Danube frontier, rebelled against the Roman Empire who ended up giving North Africa to them in the Vth c. Berber kingdoms rebelled, fought against them, and ensured a rapid fall of vandal ruling. This was then followed by Byzantin occupation, mainly limited to Ceuta and Tangier – although Byzantin remains have been also found in Salé and Volubilis. To them, these faraway frontiers of West North Africa felt too isolated: these new invasions did not last. By the end of the VIIth c., *"no external power had ever really penetrated Mauritania Tingitana deeply. Now the whole of north-western Africa awaited a new ruler"* (Pennel, 2009: 18).

The Arab invasions, Islam, and the Berbers of North Africa

Tourabi (2012: 7) stresses that

> Romans, Vandals, Byzantins, have successively invaded Morocco and stopped the resurgence of Berber kingdoms without succeeding in profoundly altering their ethnic composition, nor generating radical transformations in the Berber identity and culture. Only Islam, and successive migrations of Arab communities, succeeded in integrating themselves to the Berber identity.

Thus, it is at the end of the VIIth c. that Muslim armies pushed into North-Western Africa, where the Berber communities were organized into large federations based on cultural regional differences rather than political units. Berber societies were primarily tribal. Their resistance to Muslim invaders were literally legendary and included great figures such as that of Kahina, a Berber woman from the Aurès region in Algeria, who fought against the Arabs until she died. All in all, it took the Arabs as much time to definitely control North Africa as it did them to conquer Syria, Iran, and Spain all together. Musa ibn Nusair, the Arab governor, is credited for having established Arab rule all over North Africa by 710 (Howe, 2005: 59).

To the Berbers, a religion that was based not on birth or racial origin but upon religious commitment, was attractive. They also progressively saw in Islam a way of cementing their tribal divisions. For these reasons, they sought ways of willingly "joining the Arabs" – for instance, by becoming clients of Arab tribes, or by joining their army (which many did). However, most of the time, Berbers were forced to join the Muslims and, if defeated, their men could be sent to the East as slaves, whilst Berber women would be sent to harems where they were particularly prized.

Even when they submitted to Islam, Berbers were taxed as if they were non-Muslims. Because of this, many Berbers resented their Arab rulers treating them so unfairly, when Islam proclaimed all believers to be equal. As a consequence, in North Africa, a mixture of resistance and heterodoxy shaped the unfolding of a Maghribian Islam and, some would say, sealed the foundations of what is now viewed as the Moroccan nation. This was not done without pain: in 740, a tax revolt was led by a Berber named Maysara who declared himself caliph and started the "Khariji insurrection". A few years later:

> on the Atlantic plains, a state grew up that was so heterodox it could hardly be called Muslim at all. Sometime around 744, Salih bin Trif declared himself a prophet, wrote a holy book influenced by the Quran – but in Berber language. (…) His state, the Berghawata, had mixed elements of Christianity, Judaism and Animism onto a Shi'I base. (…) Islam did not touch large areas of central Morocco and the Atlantic plains, it preferred agricultural areas and pasture land to trade, and the religion of those Berbers who did convert was sometimes very heterodox indeed.
>
> (Pennell, 2009: 28)

Although the heterodox states represented a Berber view of Islam rather than an Arab one, the Berbers were willing to be Muslims: in fact, they insisted on having their status as Muslims recognized.

In 809, Idriss II, the son of Idriss I, founder of the Idrissid dynasty (which also had such heterodox roots), moved his capital from Volubilis to Fès, and his rule spread through the construction of little fortified townships along the main routes linking Fès, Al-Andalus, and the Arab East. Although these routes were very much used for commerce, they also helped refugees from both Cordoba and Kairouan, fleeing for political and religious reasons, to reach Fès where they settled in what became the "Kairouan quarter" and the "Andalus quarter", that both still exist in the old medina.

When, in the Xth c., the Umayyads won economic control of the Sahara gold trade against the Fatimids in Al Maghrib, which had become their battleground, their allies started controlling much of Morocco. From then on, a sunni form of Islam became the dominant religious and political framework in the country. Its prosperity, though, depended on the commerce and stability of Al-Andalus and, when Berber troops revolted against the palace in Cordoba in 1031 and made the Umayyad caliphate collapse, Morocco became redefined as an imperial centre in its own right.

The Al-Andalus contribution to indigenous North African culture

We will come back extensively to Al-Andalus when talking about water management, later in this book. But for now, it is worth explaining to what extent all that is encompassed in the term "Al-Andalus" – both a region in Southern Spain and an era, a period of scientific and cultural vibrancy, of religious tolerance, or urban development and agronomic ingenuity – had anything to do with the "indigenous people" whose water management practices we are here interested in.

Tariq Ibn Ziad, of Berber origins, famously joined the Arab army following the Muslim invasions from the East, and was even sent by Ibn Noussaïr to do nothing less than ... conquer Spain! As Al Khalili explains:

> It is after him, that JbelTariq (Tariq's mountain), the huge rock overlooking the Mediterranean, "Gibraltar", was named. The victory of his army, at the beginning of the VIIIth c., marked the beginning of the Moors' conquest of Spain as well as of eight centuries of "Al-Andalus" (...). During these centuries, Cordoba became a capital city and the most important city in Europe under the Umayyad caliphate (929–1031), then Sevilla, then Granada, whose fall in 1492 marked the apogee of the Reconquista.
>
> (Al Khalili, 2010: 189)

Whilst, in most of Europe, the Middle Ages are referred to as the "Dark ages" – times of wars, epidemics, feudal regimes, the domination of a very powerful Christian church, and ignorance – this period was also the "golden age of Arabic science". Indeed, at that time, in the Middle East ruled by the Abbassyd dynasty, as well as in Al-Andalus, a phenomenal dynamism and creativity was fuelling the translation of Greek and Sanskrit Indian scientific texts, encouraging scholarship, scientific enquiry, and exchanges, and generating advances in improving living conditions of communities, both in rural and in urban areas.

Tariq Ibn Ziad's "entry" in Europe initiated a whole set of communication and exchanges between Al-Andalus and the Middle East and, as Baghdad had its "House of Wisdom", Bayt-Al-Hikma, so did Cordoba and Toledo, with huge libraries which allowed the collection of thousands of scientific tresors, later translated from Arabic or Hebrew into Latin, and sparkling the European Renaissance.

Amongst the great contributors to this is, without doubt, the most famous of the Andalusian philosophers, Abu al-Walid Muhammad ibn Rushd (Averroes) (1126–1198), considered as the father of secular thought in Europe and one of the most important philosophers of all times. He is famous for integrating Aristotle's philosophy with Islamic theology (Al Khalili 2010: 199). The scientists of Al-Andalus also shared their engineering knowledge by showing techniques to build dams, canals, water wheels, and pumps. They were renowned for building splendid and sophisticated water clocks. They contributed to the Islamic agricultural revolution with new methods of irrigation as well as new species introduced into Europe and then North Africa by their agronomists. With the fall of Granada in 1492, the Reconquista brought most of the Andalusian centres under Christian control. Persecuted Muslims and Jewish communities fled and found refuge in North Africa. Such migration had also taken place under the Almohads, who were fanatically rigid advocates of Islam. Maimonid (Mosche ben Maimon), great philosopher, was one of the Jewish people who escaped to Morocco in the XIIth c. The impact that Al-Andalus people had on the "culture and identity" of indigenous communities of North Africa and their relationship to their natural environment is undeniable.

The great Berber dynasties

Reviewing what happened next, during the ten centuries that separate us from that period, would be too complex – albeit fascinating. Tourabi (2012) rightly asserted that "*Morocco is not exclusively Berber, Arabic, Muslim, Jewish or African… It is all of it at once – a mixture, a synthesis*" (p. 2). And indeed, as we have already seen, despite rebellions, Berbers mixed with Arabs, and history hosted and integrated various religions, refugees, and even triggered the emergence of creative religious heterodox principles. However, it is important to appreciate the extent to which dynasties such as the Almoravids, the Almohads, and the Maranids put their marks as Berber Muslim dynasties on the cultural identity of the country – as well as on water management practices, as we will see in Chapter 2.

The first ones brought unity to the patchwork of statelets that Maghrib was in the XIth c., and its trade activities reunited North-West Africa with the Almoravids ruling Tlemcen, Oran, and Algiers, as well as creating their capital city, Marrakesh, in the South of Morocco. The Muslims of Al-Andalus sought their help against Christians and the Almoravids saved Seville that then became their capital city. They

imposed themselves under the pretext that they had to protect Islam –
which they followed extremely rigorously, if not puritanically.

> What does remain of the Almoravids is the elaborate system of
> underground irrigation channels (*khettaras*) that watered gardens
> around Marrakesh and the huge defensive walls around the city –
> two projects that were hardly surprising in an empire founded by
> desert warriors.
>
> (Pennell, 2009: 47)

The Almohads (XIIth/XIIIth c.), Berbers from the mountains led
by Ibn Tumart, organized a Berber confederation in Morocco and
intervened again in Al-Andalus, where they took control of most of
Islamic Spain. The intellectual life of the Almohads was much more vig-
orous that it had been under the Almoravids. This led the Almohads to
encourage Sufism and brought to Morocco great philosophers from Al-
Andalus to Marrakesh, in particular (Muhammed Ibn Rushd – known
in Europe as Averroes). The Almohads built impressive fortresses, such
as the walls of Fès, for instance, and the gate of the Oudaya in Rabat.
They also invested heavily in irrigation works and developed sugar cane
and cotton cultivation in the Souss. Gardens surrounded most towns
and there was large-scale irrigation around Marrakech and Fès. The
Almohad economy was very dependent on commerce with Europe
and across the Sahara and, when territorial domination faltered, the
economy declined (Pennell, 2009: 54).

The following dynasty of the Marinids were Berber tribesmen. The
language of the tribes was Berber and it was also the language of the
court. The language of the law and Islamic government, however, was
Arabic. There was a constant tension between the Islamic norms and the
dynastry's needs. Consequently, the Marinids were forced to mobilize
religious support through political alliances with the two most powerful
religious groups: the *ulamas* and the *sharifs*. Learning lay at the centre
of the *ulama*'s notion of religion and the Marinids encouraged it by
importing an institution that had originated in the far East and spread
to North Africa: the *madrasa*, or residential college, where students
lived and studied. The success of the Marinid laid in creating alliances
with Berber tribes all around the country. But, as explains Pennell, it is
also under the dynasty of the Maranids, in the XIVth c., that the whole
region of the Maghrib, or North Africa, started being deunited: "*from
then on, the far west dominated by Marrakesh and Fès would be separate
from the centre, or Ifriqiya, laying the basis for the territorial distinctiveness of Morocco*" (Pennel, 2009: 64).

The fall of Granada in 1492 marked the end of Al-Andalus. After being chased from the Iberian peninsula, Moroccans were on the defensive and the XVIth c., XVIIth c., and XVIIIth c. became times of great political turmoil. Civil war always threatened, one *sharifian* regime replaced another and, ultimately, Morocco got divided. The *Saadi* controlled the Southern part of Morocco whilst the *Wattasis* controlled the North (Howe, 2005: 60). It was also a time when trade was encouraged. Thus, in 1585, Elizabeth gave the Barbary Company an exclusive monopoly of Anglo-Moroccan trade for 12 years and *Saadi* Morocco exported animal hides (tanning developed rapidly in Tetouan), metalwork (in Marrakesh) and above all sugar – whose production was located in the Tensift valley at Chichaoua and in the Souss valley. The sugar trade collapsed when the English found better quality and cheaper sugar in Brazil (Pennell, 2009: 87). When Al Mansur died of the plague (in 1603), which was raging throughout the country, Morocco disintegrated into fiefs ruled by whoever could win enough support. An agonising messy context characterizes XVIIth c. Morocco, dominated by civil wars and continuous corsairing. In the middle of it, another *sherifian* family emerged from the desert: the Alawi. They had come from Arabia and had settled in Sigilmassa in the XIIIth c. In 1668, they captured Fès, helped by local Arab tribes. Mawlay Rachid was proclaimed the first Alawi sultan, soon followed, in 1672, by Mawlay Ismail, his younger brother, who ruled Morocco for half a century (Howe, 2005: 60).

The Alawi dynasty is still ruling the country.

The Berber movement in context

To the questions "who are the indigenous people of North Africa?", numerous authors specialists of the region will unequivocally respond "the Amazigh people (Berbers)". Thus, Handaine (2016: 344) claimed a rate of 65–70% Tamazight (Berber) speaking population for North Africa, bringing the Amazigh-speaking population to around 20 million in Morocco, and 30 million throughout North Africa and the Sahel. Gagliardi (2019) described this largest ethnolinguistic groups, as a "*majoritarian minority*" (p. 2). In North Africa, and Morocco more specifically, these statistics have animated controversy. The recognition of the importance of the Amazigh people as a community, with its specific culture, language, identity, but also a heritage that could be taken into account into the strategic design of development strategies, is being discussed and questioned.

In this section, we are going to explore the "Berber movement", which started asserting itself after the independence of the country, in

1956, and which, in the last two decades, has gained a real momentum. As Al Aissati (2001: p. 63) explains, the massive campaigns recently organized by Amazigh activists have been aimed at publicizing the type of knowledge which would make Imazighen aware of their rediscovered indigenous heritage. Although the Maghrib as a whole has long been recognized as a distinct "unit of analysis" within which Berbers (Imazighen) are central, forming '*the basis of the whole North African edifice*' (Hart 1999: 23), "*in recent years, however, a modern Amazigh (literally: 'free man') identity movement has emerged with a concrete and symbolic agenda that poses fundamental challenges to North African states and societies*" (Maddy-Weitzman, 2015: 2499). Berbers are not to be "studied" anymore: they need to be both recognized and integrated into policy-making and strategies. The Amazigh current is now a component of the debates in North Africa's increasingly contested public sphere. "*The movement's agenda is both specifically Berber and 'national', favouring a genuine democratic system based on a broad social contract, rule of law, and a refashioning of the fundamentals of national identity*" (Maddy-Weitzman, 2015: 2500). The "Amazigh Cultural Movement" (ACM), a civil society movement based on the defence of universal values of human rights, has encouraged the creation of more than 800 Amazigh associations established throughout the whole of Morocco (Handaine, 2016: 344). As we will see, the emergence of the Berber movement marks a new twist in the historical constructions of social identities in the Maghrib.

Considering the importance Berber communities had in North Africa over centuries, why was there a need to initiate such a movement and why has it been so contested?

Why was the Berber movement created?

It would seem that the motivations for gathering efforts to create the Berber Movement were threefold.

Disappointments after the independence of the country in 1956

As Rollinde (1999) explains, most advocates of the Berber movement were initially marked by the disappointment of how things evolved just after the independence of the country, in 1956. To start with, the Berber Decree, or the "Dahir berbère", issued in May 1930 by the French administration, had aimed to put into place two different legal systems in Morocco: one for the Imazighen, deriving its essence from the local customary laws, and one for the Arabs, based on the Islamic law or the "Shariâa". French colonial authorities had tried to oppose the Arab-led nationalist movement by favouring Berbers. This proved counterproductive (Howe, 2005: 177): the decree was fervently opposed by both Arabs and Imazighen who saw it as a direct application of the "divide and rule" maxim, and a direct attack on the Muslim unity of the Moroccans (Al Aissati 2001: 61). Whilst the Decree ceased to apply a few years later, it had raised tensions between two communities who, originally, were willing to be united in front of the colonizer.

Another problem isolated the Berber communities from the others in Morocco, during the Protectorate period. As Handaine (2016) explains, *"a number of Amazigh tribes had [had] their land expropriated by France during the Amazigh people's resistance to colonisation. Following independence, these tribes never recovered that land, despite a number of demands and protests"* (p. 347). Just after the independence, the government, instead of returning these pieces of lands to the Amazigh communities, considered them to be State lands – and we are talking here about 12 million hectares of indigenous land (Handaine, 2016). Millions of families were moved to the cities where they attempted to integrate, find jobs, and ultimately lost their identity. Conscious of the fact that this violated rights that are guaranteed by international instruments, King Mohamed VI, in his discourse dated 8 December 2014, gave instructions to review the situation of lands known as *"sulalya lands"* (lands managed by tribes). The tribes are now waiting enthusiastically for solutions that can guarantee their rights. This issue is however still pending.

The end of the pan-Arabism movement

A second major motivation behind the creation of the Berber movement is related to the end of the Pan-Arabism movement. Ould Mohamedou (2019) described that movement as

> the story of a century – from about the great Arab revolt of 1916 until the June 1967. During that time, cultural commonalities across the Arab world and the long history of the Arab empires straddling East and West provided a ready-made basis to formulate a project meant to expel the colonisers and build new modern states while linking the Arab peoples.

Although the Pan-Arabism movement was strong and had substantial appeal in large segments of the Middle Eastern and North African world, it did not succeed. The failure of the postcolonial authoritarian Arab states became associated with the ideology they championed. A new form of pan-Arabism (one that would be less state-centred, more bottom-up, and that would emerge from better interconnections across the Arab civil society) was also noticeably present during the 2011 Arab Spring. However, for all their important regional commonalities, those revolts were primarily about local issues.

And so, it is fair to say that 1967 had already marked the end of "pan-Arabism". By then, giving priority to democracy had already become more important than giving priority to the "Arab cause". *"Many realised that political regimes aimed at 'liberating people' can often become oppressive regimes. Those started looking for a new political project that would be based on authentic cultural values. That quest would either lead to Islamism or Amazighism"* (Rollinde, 1999: 2). It is not surprising, then, that the "Berber Movement" started that same year, in 1967, with the creation of the AMREC. This "Moroccan Association on Research and Cultural Exchanges" was aimed at defending Amazigh culture and popular arts. Defending the Berber language was then considered as taboo. The link between the Amazigh language and the pan-Arabism movement is important: it is this movement which, by installing a highly arabized administrative and legal system in Morocco, Tunisia and Lybia (where Amazigh speakers have been reduced in number to a few thousands) put most pressure on Amazigh culture and way of life (IWGIUA website).

The end of pan-Arabism therefore opened doors to reconsidering how citizens of a same country could live together, and in which languages people could communicate, decide, and express laws.

> Since the death of Morocco's King Hassan II, one of the strongest defenders of pan-Arabism in the region, and the ascension of his son Mohammed VI to the helm of power, Amazighité has become increasingly recognised for its contribution to Moroccan identity on a social, cultural and academic level.
>
> (Jay, 2016: 68)

Intellectual revival of the 90s

In the 1990s, a genuine rebirth of the Amazigh movement could be observed in Morocco. One of the prime initial motivation for it was to promote the recognition of the status of the Amazigh language, known to be the indigenous language of the populations of North Africa for over 30 centuries. As Al Aissati explained, "*the most prominent index to ethnicity is linguistic. People define themselves as Imazighen once they speak the Amazigh. Once the speaker ceases to speak Amazigh, there remains little about him which would indicate his 'Amazighness'*" (p. 58, 59).

The Amazigh revival movement also became a central issue in political and cultural debates in the second half of the XXth c.: it is at that time that the Amazigh intellectual movement obtained tools such as linguistic theories, to redefine his own social group in positive terms. When Amazigh readers started reading texts on the history of North-Africa, old Numidia under the Roman rule, or on the origin and native language of some glorious empires, they rediscovered their own historical heritage, a source of pride and inspiration to many cultural and political activists. "*This historical dimension constituted a direct challenge to the precepts of Islam, which stipulate that history begins with Islam; before Islam was the period of ignorance and savagery*" (Al Aissati 2001: 60).

Hassen Id Belkacem, the director of the Berber journal Tasafut, was the main man behind the ANCAP (Association Nouvelle pour la Culture et les Arts Populaires), created in 1978. It was thanks to him that the Berber movement, originally focused on culture, moved on to defending Amazigh rights and appeared in front of international organisms (Rollinde, 1999: 2). In 1979, the creation of AMDH (Moroccan Association on Human Rights) was followed by the organization of the 1980 Agadir Summer University on "Popular Culture: unity emerging from diversity".

After the social uprisings in Casablanca, in 1981, the Berber movement was obliged to stop all of its activities until the end of the 1980s. Some Amazigh journals were forbidden. "*One of the leaders who dared claim that Tamazight is a language on a par with Arabic was sentenced to a year in prison. This was at the height of the 'Années de plomb', when human rights were meaningless*" (Howe, 2005: 178).

The creation of the OMDH (Moroccan Organisation of Human Rights) in 1988 and the Golf War facilitated the reintroduction of the Amazigh movement which, with the August 1991 Agadir Charter (considered as the first political act of the Berber movement (Howe, 2005: 178), created the "first national declaration of the cultural movement". The charter called for a democratic linguistic and cultural policy, based on the recognition of the legitimate linguistic and cultural rights of all members of the Moroccan people. It formulated some requests (revendications), including that of having the Constitution reviewed in view of recognizing the national character of the Amazigh language side by side with the arabic language (Rollinde, 1999: 4).

However, despite high hopes and much effort, the revival of a Berber renaissance, in the 1990s, was not a unified movement.

> It is characterised by the plurality of its objectives, strategies and groups representing it. Initiated amongst university movements (in particular through the UNEM – Union of Moroccan Students), it progressively asserted itself through artistic initiatives and developed its NGO strategies which, for some of them, went beyond national borders and evolved into the creation of political parties.
>
> (Rollinde, 1999: 2)

Current state of affairs

Recognition of the Berber identity in Morocco – the 2011 Constitution

As Maddy-Weitzman (2015: 2502) explained, "*the Amazigh element was very much part of the initial Arab-Spring protests in early 2011*". Amazigh activists prominently displayed their movement's flag and advocated full linguistic and cultural recognition within a reformed "parliamentary monarchy", focusing both on national issues and local specific needs. The Riffian Berber tribes, who live in the neglected, rugged north, carried longstanding grudges against the monarchy. They had already formed alliances with urban elites before the independence. King Mohamed VI knew that and, quickly after ascending the throne in July 1999, quickly moved to begin repairing the breach between the region and state authorities, acting on both the symbolic and practical levels. Nonetheless, true integration and reconciliation was far from achieved.

Changes in the Constitution, in 2011, helped in doing so: the new text thus asserted the principle of equality between men and women (art. 19) and officialized the (indigenous) Amazigh language (art. 5) alongside Arabic (Gagliardi 2019: 1). As Maddy Weitzman (2015) stressed

> it emphasized that the Amazigh people and culture constituted an integral component of Moroccan identity, which had been forged over the course of history alongside the Arab-Islamic and Saharan-Hassanian components and enriched along the way by African, Andalusian, Hebraic and Mediterranean currents. The Constitution explicitly recognised Tamazight as an official state

language, alongside Arabic, making Morocco the only North African state, and only the second core Arab League member state (after Iraq), in which Arabic was not the sole official language.

(p. 2502)

However, as Handaine stressed (2016), work to harmonize the legal arsenal with the new Constitution has not, in fact, been fully achieved yet.

Going beyond – globalization, post Arab-Spring, and fighting Islamism

Various factors helped the Amazigh movement to regain momentum and recognition, not only at a national but also at a global level.

Firstly, various events (International Conference of Human Rights in Vienna, 1993; the Douarnenez congress in France, in August 1994, as well as the speech given at the UN by Hassen Id Belkacem, during the launch of the Decade of Autochtone people, in December 1994) allowed to internationalize the Amazigh question. The Preparation of the Amazigh World Congress was held in Lozère, in 1995, and gathered personalities representing the whole of the Maghreb and of the Sahel (Maroc, Algérie, Libye, Mauritanie, Mali, Niger), Canary Islands, and also Europe and America. It is during that event that a proposal to create a permanent international NGO (World Amazigh Congress) was made, to be completed by an international internet forum.

Secondly, in 2000, a group of Berber intellectuals made public the Berber Manifesto which went beyond cultural demands, accused their Arab compatriots of ideological hegemony aimed at ethnocide and of falsifying history in favour of the Arabs, and stressed the marginalization of Berber areas (Howe, 2005: 179).

Thirdly, in the aftermath of the 2003 Casablanca terrorist bombings, the monarchy and Amazigh militants formed an alliance against Islamists (Becker, 2009: 149). Using the momentum created by the Arab Spring revolutions, Amazigh militants took advantage of the media focus on the 20th February movement and on other groups to raise their own profile. Amazigh flags showed again that Amazighity had become a form of cultural resistance against both the traditional Moroccan state built on Arabo-Islamic values, and the growing influence of Islamist parties. As Jay concludes, *"Through globalisation, the development of the Internet, and social networking, the Berber Renaissance hence drew the attention of audiences from North Africa and beyond, united around a new, homogeneous concept of Amazighity"* (2016: 69).

Conclusion

The importance of the Amazigh people of Morocco and their indigenous nature is not questioned anymore. The fact that the 2011 Constitution officially recognized the Amazigh identity and language is a very positive and encouraging step forward for the Amazigh people of Morocco. Unfortunately, there is still a lot to be done to harmonize the legal arsenal with the constitution. Moroccan Amazigh have carried on referring to the original Berber society as a model of democracy and have been the fervent advocates of an "authentic discourse" which is not imported from the West. The objective kept on being to mark a clear divide between them and the colonial reference to the Berber Dahir and *"to suggest an alternative to the Arabic nation by putting forward another type of 'common nation'"* (Rollinde, 1999: 5).

Despite a positive response from King Mohamed the VIth, who, for instance, created the Royal Institute of Amazigh Culture in 2003 (Jay, 2016), official recognition of the importance of the Amazigh culture still needs to be reinforced. In 2007, Morocco did not ratify ILO Convention 169 and did not vote in favour of the UNDRIP in 2007 (IWGIUA website).

If the Berber movement is to gain importance and legitimacy and if, even more importantly, it is to reach out and represent in its advocacy and institutions even remote components of rural constituencies, including rural women, it needs to move away from mainly being "top-down, urban elites, intelligentsia-driven" (Gagliardi, 2019). As Silverstein highlights, *"despite the growing political influence of Amazigh groups, rural populations who occupy the Amazigh heartland are often left disempowered and 'accuse activists of ignoring local problems and of prioritising, instead, abstract issues'"* (2013: 774).

What this book suggests to initiate is a type of defence of indigenous heritage that will highlight the value and the centrality of the Berber heritage in the current context of climate change and water stress. This is presenting us with constraints and obstacles that require resilience and adaptability – the type of qualities that policymakers would benefit from learning from people who have closely interacted with their natural arid and semi-arid environment and have survived and thrived within it.

References

Al Khalili, J. (2010) *Path finders; the Golden Age of Arabic science.* London: Penguin Books.

Becker, C. (2009) Art, Self-censorship and Public Discourse: Contemporary Moroccan Artists at the Crossroads. *Contemporary Islam.* 3 (2): 143–166.

El Aissati, A. (2001) Ethnic identity, language shift and the Amazigh voice in Morocco and Algeria. *Race, Gender and Class.* 8 (3): 57–69.

Gagliardi, S. (2019) Indigenous peoples' rights in Morocco: subaltern narratives by Amazigh women. *The International Journal of Human Rights.* 23 (1): 281–296.

Handaine, M. (2016) Morocco. In Vinding and Mikkelsen (Eds). *The Indigenous world 2016.* Copenhagen: IWGIA, pp. 344–348. www.iwgia. org/en/news-alerts/archive?view=article&id=718:indigenous-peoples-in-morocco&catid=167 accessed on 04th of June 2020.

Hart, D. (1999) Scratch a Moroccan, Find a Berber. *Journal of North African Studies.* 4 (2): 23–26.

Howe, M. (2005) *Morocco. The Islamist awakening and other challenges.* Oxford: Oxford University Press.

Jay, C. (2016) Playing the 'Berber': the performance of Amazigh identities in contemporary Morocco. *Journal of North African Studies.* 21(1): 68–80.

Maddy-Weitzman, B. (2015) A turning point? The Arab Spring and the Amazigh movement. *Ethnic and Racial Studies.* 38 (14): 2499–2515.

Ould Mohamedou, M.M. (2019) The rise and fall of pan-Arabism, interview by Aditya Kiran Kakati. https://graduateinstitute.ch/communications/news/rise-and-fall-pan-arabism, accessed on 15th of September 2020.

Pennell, C.R. (2009) *Morocco. From empire to independence.* Oxford: OneWorld.

Rollinde, M. (1999) Le mouvement Amazigh au Maroc: défense d'une identité culturelle, revendication du droit des minorités ou alternative politique? *Insaniyat, Revue algérienne d'anthropologie et de Sciences Sociales.* 8: 63–70.

Silverstein, P. A. (2013) The Pitfalls of Transnational Consciousness: Amazigh Activism as a Scalar Dilemma. *Journal of North African Studies.* 18 (5): 768–778.

Tourabi, A. (2012) Histoire : le Maroc avant l'Islam, *TelQuel,* 12 Aout, N.907 https://telquel.ma/2012/08/12/histoire-le-maroc-avant-lislam_1084, accessed on 04th of June 2020.

2   A mixed heritage of traditional water management systems

Water is life: hygiene, spirituality, and beauty

The tradition of thermal baths and the birth of great cities

All around the Mediterranean Basin, Greek and Roman civilizations have left their marks in terms of water management. Whilst the Greeks greatly contributed to the structuration of public spaces, the Romans helped in transporting water to and from urban centres. As is the case in Islam, water had a sacred value and was present in Greek and Roman temples, as it is in mosks. Besides, the well-known tradition of "waters that heal", or thermal baths from the Antiquity, also existed in North Africa. In Morocco, Moulay Yacoub, Sidi Harazem, and Aiin Chkef are good examples of such sites that are still in use and well-known for helping cure diseases such as skin diseases, fragile nervous systems, conjunctivitis, and even liver and kidney malfunctions (Secret, 1990: 93).

These sites are located in the region of Fès, founded by the Idrissid dynasty. For Berber speakers, the name Fès actually originates from the term *nfas*, or spillway, and illustrates how rich in water, springs, and rivers, the region is. If "water is life", certain waters have particular powers and, in the case of Moulay Yacoub, great legends were told that link the medicinal powers of water to the prestige that emerged from the areas. The name of Moulay Yacoub derives from Louba, great Berber king living under Roman occupation, whose capital was Volubilis. He had studied medicine in Rome and brought back with him the Greek doctor Euphorbos, specialized in waters that heal. Together, they contributed to the building of the aqueduct that helped bring the sulphurous waters of Moulay Yacoub to Volubilis. Arabic historians also explain how the Almohad Sultan Yacoub El Mansour (XIIth c.), who was suffering from terrible ulcers, could only be cured by the waters of Moulay Yacoub. This led him to build the first thermal baths on the site. Doctor Edmond Secret, specialized in thermal waters in Morocco, explained how:

> in the old days, people had developed hygienic rules that would incite them to first drink rain water, then, in second place, spring water that would have flown onto a red soil and last, water from a spring. Water coming from a well was drank last.
>
> (Secret, 1990: 75)

The selection of sites to build prestigious cities such as Fès in the IXth c. was thus highly influenced by the presence of water. Then, a mixed heritage of Greek, Roman, Berber, and Middle Eastern ingenuity helped to optimize the use of water in what became thriving cities. Authors such as Henri Gaillard (In Michel, 2016) have highlighted how water contributed to the wealth of the city. He explains that:

> all authors who described [the Arab city] have admired the abundance of its irrigation system. Even the poorest households enjoyed a plentiful of water. (…) Through an irrigation system put in place by the first Berber dynasties and then improved by the Almoravids and the Almohads, clean, drinkable water was brought to the city by canals and a sewage system took dirty water to a specific area of the city. Dams and water towers were later built by the Maranid dynasty.
>
> (p. 201, 202)

Serrhini (2003) explains that this three-water-networks system was in use until the XIXth c.

The first network transporting clean water (not drinkable by humans) was used to clean houses, irrigate allotments and gardens, artisanal activities (tannery and dye industry), and to activate mills thanks to gravity (Privitera and Metalsi, 2016). The second network was transporting, via a pottery canal system, the *maâda*, drinkable water distributed to private houses and some 70 public fountains. The third network, the *sloukia*, took dirty water to the Sebou river, outside town. At the time, the size of the network was sufficient for the size of the population, and the waste taken outside the city had enough time to naturally biodegrade.

As we will see, things have since changed.

Water in Islamic architecture

Fountains

If the tradition of public fountains is so widespread in North Africa, it is because it allows to fulfil one of the main duty of Islam: to provide water freely for all. Fountains already existed in Greek Antiquity as central components of public spaces. As Viviers (2017) notices, Greek societies used urban fountains, especially monumental ones, to illustrate social status and power. In a country like Morocco, public fountains (*seqqayas*) are often sumptuously decorated and constitute a distinctive component of the street or a *souk* (public market). They are often mural fountains with a vertical back that is entirely decorated with multicoloured *zelliges* (mosaiques).

Under the Almohad dynasty, Fès had no less than 80 such *seqqayas*. In Marrakesh, in the South of Morocco, it is partly thanks to the construction of fountains that the Saady dynasty managed to regain popularity and to make the city brilliant again until the middle of the XVIIth c. To do so, they found an ally in water: architects and water engineers focused their talents on building spectacular fountains accessible to all citizens, restoring city gardens and reconnecting the city with the exterior, in particular by repairing the main city bridges.

Hammams and the surrounding urban fabric

It is true that the North African *hammam* has inherited from the Roman and Greek tradition of public baths. In the Antiquity, private hygiene was a very public affair indeed! However, whilst the tradition of the public baths has largely been lost in many parts of the Northern Mediterranean shore, it is still very much alive in North Africa and, in particular in Morocco where going to the *hammam* is a very common habit, practiced by all social classes. Studies have shown that, in Fès, in the XIIth c. under the dynasty of the Almohads, there were 93 *hammams*. When the Maranid dynasty took over, they boosted this tradition even more (Terrasse, 1954; Secret, 1990). In 1999–2000, 30 *hammams* still functioned in the old medina of Fès (Sibley, 2006).

Historians specialized in Islamic architecture have shown how the structure of current *hammams* in the Islamic world has moved away from the Roman style in order to integrate Muslim practices. Secret (1990) explains that:

> Idriss II, who founded Fès, brought to it the practice of the roman bath from Volubilis – where ruins of Roman thermal bath can still

be seen. The architecture of the hammams clearly reveals how the moor baths come from the Roman baths. However, the moor baths got rid of all luxurious characteristics. Whilst Muslim architecture is normally characterised by a set of rooms around an open space, the patio, the hammam is linear with rooms following each other "in the Roman way".

(Secret, 1990: 57, 58)

Besides, in the moor *hammam*, the Roman cold pool disappears: following Muslim principles, one needs to wash in water that is non-stagnant.

Sibley (2006) has described the *hammam* as a particular" service", fully integrated in the urban fabric. It does encourage the respect of individual hygiene (the *hammam* is located close to the mosque where one goes and prays once clean) and the cleanliness of public places. It uses natural resources in an efficient way. Water is consumed in very precise quantities. Fuel heats up the water but the heat hence generated is also used in the communal *ferran* (public oven). Both *hammam*s and public ovens serve as meeting points in the neighbourhood.

Water clocks

These are worth mentioning, as they are still visible in some urban locations, although in disuse. They originated from the Middle East where many engineers viewed their scientific knowledge as worth being used in the creation of beautiful objects such as clocks.

Al Jazari, engineer and inventor of the XIIth c., was such a polymath scientist. He built the famous "elephant clock" that fascinated so many of his colleagues. It was a weight powered water clock in the form of an Asian elephant which used technologies derived from Indian, Persian, and Chinese clocks, expressing the multicultural mentality of his creator. As we will see in later sections, the notion of time also became important in traditional water management, as it helped in doing nothing less than managing conflicts between water users.

Islamic architecture and water

Islamic architecture entertains a specific relationship to water: water is central to the *riad*, or central court around which habitations gravitate. Aguillar et al. (2014), who describe the *riad* as a sustainable architecture structure, explain that:

the adoption of the riad in the Islamic world is due to the fact that it perfectly fits social, cultural and environmental principles of Islam (...). The centrality of the patio facilitates the natural ventilation of habitable spaces thanks to the physical properties of air: warm air, less dense than cold air, rises.

(p. 551)

The presence of water in the central courtyard ensures that the house is kept cool. Most of the time, the central fountain generates a pleasant musicality in an enclosed garden, itself generating a micro-climate. Hence the heavenly garden, so dear to desert people amongst whom Islam was born, is brought all the way home.

City gardens

Traditionally in Islam, gardens represent the image of what is even more beautiful than life: paradise. The symbolism behind the garden is therefore considerable. As Benchaâbane (2014) emphasizes:

in Islam, all gardens emerged from desert sands and from the hard work of God's gardeners; they all symbolise the hope for creating heaven on earth. (...) The Qu'ran describes *Al Firdaws*, heaven, as a garden crossed by four rivers. (...) Meditation in a garden, as well as the contemplation of the water-mirror, invites one to the divine sphere.

(p. 25, 26)

Whilst the first type of urban Islamic garden is the patio, the second one is found in subsistence agriculture allotments. These first appeared in Tunis, with the Kairouan School and the great water reservoirs of the Aghlabide dynasty, where vast orchards called *agdals* were organized in large squares of cultivated land, separated by irrigation canals and sometimes comprising a pavilion in the middle, giving it a unique aesthetic aspect. In fact, the art of the Arabo-Islamic garden evolved for nearly 6000 years. It was strongly inspired by Persian gardens, themselves embellished, from an agronomical perspective, by the various contributions of Turkish, Celtic, Roman, Greek, Indian, Mongol, and even Chinese people. These contributions went hand in hand with scientific and technical advances that flourished between the VIIIth c. and the IXth c. in the Middle East and Al-Andalus and contributed to the creation of hydraulic science, the development of agronomic principles and treaties, the study of botanics, the creation of great parks, and the birth of landscape gardening and urbanism. For Benchaâbane, there is no doubt that:

> the architecture of arabic cities – some of which became urban metropolis and capital cities of empires – viewed the garden as a key contributor to their development. Historians of the cities of the Middle Ages explain that, everywhere, the model of the garden-city prevailed. From Damas to Bagdad and from Cordoba to Marrakesh, houses appear as lost cubes in an ocean of greenery.
>
> (2014: 34)

In Marrakesh, the Agdal garden and the Ménara gardens still illustrate the tradition of the city-garden. After the fall of Granada in 1492, which marks the end of Al-Andalus, Marrakesh welcome the last Moorish communities expelled from Spain. The Almoravid dynasty created the first main orchard of Marrakech. The following dynasty (the Almohads) created another huge 550 hectares city-garden called the Agdal, in which 8 orchards and a sugar plant could be found. The Agdal was a clear illustration of the implementation of new advances in agronomy coming from Al-Andalus and, in particular, of the "tropicalization" of Mediterranean gardens. The irrigation of this immense orchard was made possible thanks to the diversion of the river Aghmat in the high Atlas and to the transport of its waters through underground canals, the *khettaras*. They also created the well-known 100 hectares Ménara garden and made the creation of *agdals* (small-scale subsistence allotments) a custom.

Water and food security

The Arab agricultural revolution

The heritage of indigenous people in terms of water management, beside urban water management, also very much relates to the production of food in urban and rural areas. In North Africa and Morocco in particular, indigenous people were originally nomadic people. With the creation of the Berber kingdoms, the roman invasions and Phoenician trading ports, people started settling and learning how to cultivate crops, including in mountainous areas.

Berber communities probably learnt directly from their Arab invaders, some of which already knew techniques such as terracing, practiced in the mountainous regions of Yemen. The Islamic expansion of the

Umayyads brought new species coming from India such as rice, citrus fruits, cotton, and spinach. They also encouraged the intensification of agriculture. Watson (1974) concluded that the expansion of Islam was not only based on urban expansion and commercial exchanges but also on a true agricultural revolution, based on technical and social changes. The Almohad and Maranid dynasties attributed power to those who can master water management. For this reason, they invited and protected water engineers and agronomists from Al-Andalus, and gave them the same privileges than they would to their military advisors. It is certainly from them that the greatest contribution to water management and the production of food comes.

The knowledge they brought was itself a mixed one. As El Faiz (2015) explains, three books compile all together the foundations of Andalusian agriculture and water management:

> Kitâb al-filaha al-rûmiyya, attributed to Qustus, as well as Kitâb filâhat al-ard, compiled by Vindânyuniûs Anatolius of Berytos in the IVth c., synthesise the greco-byzantine and Greco-roman contributions. Kitâb al filâha al nabatiyya describes the principles of Nabatean agrciculture (Mesopotamia, North West of Arabia).
>
> (El Faiz, 2015: 34)

Famous agronomy treaties also emerged from what authors described as the apogee of Arabo-Andalus water engineering and of agronomy schools (during the Xth c.). This very particular scientific era found great energy and inspiration through the translation into Arabic of the pre-mentioned books, but also through progress made in medicine and botanical studies carried out in Cordoba (IXth–Xth c.). In addition, urban growth considerably raised the issue of the food security of cities of Al-Andalus, and hence stimulated research activities that would promote agricultural activity and its outputs. In addition to these determining factors, El Faiz (2015: 19) also noticed that the agronomy movement benefited from the positive effects of political decentralization. "*In Al Andalus*", he stresses, "*irrigation was never practiced on a large scale basis and the control of water by authoritarian method was never considered as necessary*".

It is now well recognized that we inherited drop irrigation techniques from Mesopotamian civilizations. Greek scientists were particularly talented at exploiting underground water, generating ingenious grafts on fruit trees and artistically combining vegetables and flowers in allotments. Nabatean farmers knew a great deal about the salinity of soil and fertilizers. "*Numerous indicators converge to assert that*

Arabo-Andalusian agricultural activities generated high outputs" (El Faiz, 2015: 148). Besides, agronomists from Al-Andalus were well-known for mixing science and art, hence developing a real integrated rural philosophical approach of the relationship between humans and nature.

For Watson, the Arab world really innovated in the domain of irrigation from the VIIIth c. on, when new types of small dams, *norias*, and other techniques were developed. Instructions on how to build underground water channels (*qanats*, in Persia, or *khettaras* in North Africa) were thus thoroughly detailed in the Treaty of underground water exploitation (Kitab inbat al-miyyah al khafiyya) written by Al-Karaji in 1017 (El Faiz, 2015: 231). The Arabic Hydraulic School also detailed how to capture atmospheric water, build wells, save water, develop soil restoration techniques, or design water laws to regulate groundwater consumption. Azar (2000: 164) talks of an in-depth knowledge of various types of rain by the Arab agronomists, to be used or captured in various ways to increase agricultural outputs. The damages that winds can cause to crops were also very well-known.

Irrigation techniques: seguias and norias

Lifting the water to the level of the field

Water engineers from the Middle East excelled at finding ways to ensure that cities such as Baghdad (which, in the Xth c., counted some 1.5 million inhabitants) could be provided with clean water. They worked on some techniques developed by the Greeks to lift water from the river onto a higher point (using, in particular, Archimede's screw) from which it could then be distributed. In the VIIIth c., they also introduced the *noria*, a wheel activated by the circular movement of an animal that allows the lifting of water to help irrigate fields. As Azar (2000: 162) explained, this original *noria* was based on a "carrousel" mechanism based on a transmission mechanism linking a big and a small wooden wheels. In this case, water is lifted from a well. The larger *noria*, inspired by the Romans, resembles the ones built by the Muslim Moors of Al-Andalus. In Toledo, in particular, one can still see a magnificent *noria* that lifts water from 42 metres below, in order to irrigate gardens and orchards. In addition to bringing water to a site, norias were used in close conjunction with artful irrigation systems. As Azar highlighted, these implied a systemic understanding of the growth and maturing cycle of each species and *"the success of a crop therefore depended on experience, observation, and a whole set of skills that would help recover a harvest in a way that other agricultural techniques could not"* (Azar, 2000: 168).

Surface irrigation channels: the séguias

Traditionally, another system of surface water distribution is well-known in Morocco and still very much in use. It consists in a network of *seguias*, main system of collection, distribution, and transfer of surface water. In The Haouz plain, 150,000 hectares are irrigated by 140 km of *seguias* and 1000 km of smaller water channels derived from the *seguias* and called *mesrf*.

Seguias are organized in the shape of fish bones, the *seguia* being the "main bone" from which the *mesrefs* get the water to be distributed further from the river to the fields that need to be irrigated.

The water loss generating from the water infiltration in the soil can be quite high, reaching 50% of the water being transported. This "loss" is, however, intentional: some water needs to be available downstream, since some small reservoirs capture most of the available water upstream. Whilst old *seguias* allowed this infiltration, new ones, built in cement, do not. This represents a distributional problem between the upstream and downstream communities.

Managing water, working with nature

Capturing and storing water: wells and reservoirs

The tradition of rainwater storage and water reservoirs is numerous centuries old and exists everywhere in the world. In the Antiquity, water reservoirs were found in cities and in individual houses. Water reservoirs and small dams dating from Roman, Greek, and Byzantine times can still be found in various places in North Africa.

In Volubilis, in Morocco, as Panetier and Limane (2002) explain, water reservoirs were used by the Romans to regulate the pressure of water circulating in the aqueducts. From these water reservoirs, other channels, built in ceramic, took water to houses or public establishments. At the entrance, taps made in bronze allowed to control the quantity of water used by each house, and hence to calculate the water taxes to be paid to local authorities. In southern oasis of Morocco, water reservoirs are still in use, although not always well looked after.

Transporting water: aqueducts and khettaras

The Roman contribution to water management largely focused on bringing water to the cities. During colonial times in North Africa, numerous archaeological research projects helped revealed water heritage dating from the Roman times.

These notably included aqueducts – such as the aqueduct built in 130 to link the Zaghouan spring to Carthage (now Tunis) and facilitate the construction of Antonin's thermal baths, or the aqueduct of Cherchell which could transport up to 40 000 cubic meter/ day to Caesarea of Mauritania.

(Pérennès, 1993: 78)

Magnificent "Andalusian" aqueducts were also described by the Arab geographer Al-Idrissi that were located in Mérida, Segovia, Tarragone, and also in Tolèdo.

The Roman water engineering approach is thus illustrated all throughout North Africa, from Djemila, Timgad, Tipasa in Algeria, to Volubilis in Morocco. Panetier and Limane (2002), specialized in the study of Volubilis, showed that an aqueduct was constructed there at the end of the second century. It captured spring water, 1 km away from the city, reaching the centre of the city in two major public fountains. A canalization system, of more than a metre deep, covered with "paving stones" allowed the used water to be taken away from the city. In Fès, remnants of an impressive aqueduct, built at the end of the XIIIth c. can still be seen in the left wall of Bab Makina, which used to be a weapon factory in the XIXth c.

The Romans understood well the notion of gravity and how to calculate slopes, the strength of vaults, how to waterproof reservoirs. This urban focus did not mean that the Romans neglected irrigation matters. It would seem that irrigated agriculture was located in periurban areas, where cultivated areas were small-subsistence fields (Pérennès, 1993: 79).

As Azar (2000: 162–169) stresses, the water transportation system by aqueducts was later replaced by underground canalisations (*khettaras*) to avoid evaporation, hence adapting a system to the natural environment of the Arabic world.

These *khettaras* have been described by Lightfoot (1996) as underground aqueducts designed to capture underground water and transport it to surface channels aimed at transporting water to fields and communal wells. The objective is to use gravity to help the water flow but also, above all, to avoid evaporation. For the Almoravid dynasty, using the *khettaras* became the ideal way of bringing water from the snowy Atlas mountains to their new capital city based in the Haouz plain, Marrakesh.

Researchers who worked on *khettaras* agree to assert that it is in Morocco that the most spectacular network of *khettaras* still exist. In the 1980s, a network of 6000 *khettaras* (covering 900 km) could be seen in the Haouz Plain whilst 400 others existed in the Tafilalt and Souss regions, further south. The *khettaras* were the only means of irrigation on which framers could count until the beginning of the 1970s, when the government introduced new water management systems.

People and water: managing water conflicts

Traditionally in Morocco, prior to the Protectorate, water management was essentially based on a set of customary laws focused on water distribution. Ziyad (2017) explains that the main customary institution is the concept of *Jmaa,* which was put in place to deal with irrigation needs and to strengthen social control and solidarity in all its dimensions, upstream and downstream a river.

> This is because irrigation has always been a source of conflicts between the various tribes. In order to improve it, systems have been put into place to collect rain water, to deviate the flow of water (*naoura*), and to transport and distribute surface water through *seguias* and *khettaras*.
>
> (2017: 40)

In order to avoid conflicts, a system of alternative usages of the *seguia* was put in place, predicated on the establishment of a set of agreements between the tribes that share a same river. This type of agreements lead to the creation of two types of *seguias*. The *melk seguias* (around 60%) allow people to privately own the water whilst, in the context of the public *seguias* (around 40%), the order in which the *seguia* is being used follows the topography of the terrain; farmers take it in turn during a specific period of time. In both cases, an *amazzal* ensures that the distribution is fair and equitable, and is trusted to manage potential conflicts.

In the case of the *khettaras*, it was agreed by the community that the network should be built and maintained by specialist workers. In Marrakesh, those were called the *khatatiriya* and lived in Derb Toudgha (the name of the oasis the workers were coming from).

The "opening" of the *khettara* onto a *seguia* is a matter of water distribution and must be decided and controlled by the *Nouba* system following which the irrigation of fields is taken in turn. Honest, elderly men who are wise, knowledgeable, and can be trusted, were often chosen as *Mazzan* to be the "guardians of water" and to manage potential conflicts related to this distribution (Benchaâbane, 2014). This role was transmitted from father to son.

Authors specialized on water conflict management in arid environments, such as Wolf (2000), Pérennès (1993), and Ziyad (2017) were struck by methods used by Moroccan Berbers. They notice that, to solve water conflicts, Berbers have developed methods based on:

- **The distribution of time instead of a certain quantity of water**: people enjoy a time of irrigation or can, in certain instances, buy a period of time to irrigate their field. As Wolf explained, Berbers found the idea of buying water both repugnant and contrary to the principles of Islam.
- **Priorities given to certain water usage**: this method is used in constraining situations where water availability constantly changes. In Islam, priority is given to people to drink, then to animals, then irrigation is taken into consideration followed by the use of water for mills. The last priority is given to water used for irrigation and made available via modern means (pumps, etc.).
- **The protection of downstream water users**: - taken care of since upstream users could be tempted to use too much water. This is prevented by the distribution of irrigation time laps, and regional laws that forbid the usage of modern materials such as cement in the construction of *seguias*.
- **The respect for designated, trusted, negotiators**: the *alam*, also called *amazzal*, negotiate the best solutions to a water conflict and is in charge of identifying the amount of irrigation time to be allocated. He also organizes the *sulkha*, the forgiving ceremony, once the disputes have been solved. In cities, specialists regulated the distribution of water too. In Fès, they were called the *qanawiyyum*, and managed a 70-km network of water channels.

Islamic water management principles

Reference is often made to the contribution of the " 'Muslim" agronomists of Al-Andalus, when exploring traditional water management systems in use in urban and rural areas of North Africa. As we have already discovered and as we will carry on doing throughout this book, the water heritage of indigenous people in this region went in fact all the way back to Greek and Roman, Byzantine and Berber dynasties. Despite this, some elements that are characteristic of indigenous water management practices in North Africa and Morocco are directly derived from Islam. We will identify what they are in this section.

Islam was born at the end of the VIIth c. in the toughest geographical area of Western Arabia, in the trade city of Mekka. The Arab tribes living in that part of the world were mainly nomadic, and had learned to search for water for themselves and their animals. Those who had settled in the mountains of Yemen had learnt irrigated agriculture in terraces. As Azar explains:

> Islam, as a monotheist religion, fascinated non-Arab populations who were looking for renewal. In territories conquered by the Arabs, the big domains changed hands and conquering populations introduced irrigation and new agricultural methods. Peasants converted to Islam and started speaking Arabic whilst Berbers resisted and kept their customs and languages. Because cities were built along trade journeys and Muslims were encouraged to pray together in mosks, cities started representing meeting and trading points – the modern core dimension of Islam.
>
> (2000: 21)

The Umayyad dynasty secured control of the Islamic Empire that stretched over a vast area of land, from India in the East to the Atlantic Ocean in the West (Al Khalili, 2010: 26). One hundred years after they had marched out of Arabia, they reached Poitiers in 732, and then were pushed back South. There, they settled in what they created as "Al-Andalus", within which various religions cohabitated. Some people converted to Islam, some Christians and Jewish people learnt Arabic. From this, emerged a truly multicultural and multireligious community. The Abbassid dynasty (mid-VIIIth c.) took over from the Umayyad dynasty (VIIth c.). It is under their domination that scientific activities became particularly vibrant, with Greek and Sanskrit scientific texts being translated and then scientific research being encouraged by Caliphs such as Harun Al Rashid (766–809). During that era, scientific research greatly contributed to the improvement of agriculture and water management.

Houria Tazi Sadeq, specialized on water law in Morocco, emphasizes the need to appreciate the religious approach to water issues in order to understand better what was done and what could be improved, when preparing for the looming water crisis. She explains that:

> beside modern laws, the religious tradition carries on having a role to play in managing the relationships between stakeholders. (...) Each Moroccan Constitution has asserted that, in Morocco, Islam is a state religion which guaranties the free cult practice for all.
>
> (2006: 37)

Quoting the religious texts, she (2006: 38, 39) highlights the fact that Islam's approach to water gives it certain functions:

- First, water is the main source of life. The texts remind us that it is thanks to water that plants, animals, and human beings are alive and various "versets" indicate how to manage this precious resource. Similarly, it attracts the attention of Muslims on the value of water when asking *"Have you paid attention to the quantity of water you drink? Are you responsible for it falling from the clouds or is it us? If so was our will we could transform it into 'saumatre' water: why aren't you grateful?"* (Sourate Al-Furqan, 25, verset 48 et 49).

- Second, water purifies and this is why Muslims must respect the "ablution rite" when presenting themselves before God and praying.

- Third, water is a natural habitat that must be protected. In Islam, human–environment interactions are guided by the principle of *khulafas*, following which humans are the guardians of the earth.

- Finally, water must be shared. As Sourate El Qamar (54), verset 28 declares, *"Inform them that the water from their reservoirs must be shared amongst themselves"*. Whether water usage is private or public, in situations of water abundance or shortage, everybody, without discrimination, must be able to consume water in enough quantity and without waste.

Islam forbids the overconsumption of water by some people to the detriment of the community. If the quality of water is jeopardized, the person who degraded it must repair the damage caused.

As Faruqui et al. (2001) stressed, these principles have strong implications in terms of how to manage water in the XXIst c. Thus, even in the context of a modern economy, a real Muslim is not allowed to keep excess water for himself. Water rights need to respect Islamic priority (i.e., humans first, animals second, and irrigation in third position). Islamic principles stipulate that water should not be sold nor bought and that, if a system of water pricing is put into place, it should be equitable. In terms of governance, the authors finally show that consultation with all on water issues, including women, is compulsory. At the international level, the *hadiths* forbid to generate harm to other countries and to the natural environment. Finally, muslim principles specify that the *"shura"* (consultation on issues of mutual interest) and *"fassad"* (damage and aggression) should systematically be applies.

Berber characteristics in traditional water management

Although the Arabo-Muslim contribution to water management in North Africa and, in particular, Morocco, is well-recognized, it is important to appreciate the Berber origin of some characteristic indigenous practices. Authors such as El Faiz (2015), Pérennès (1993), and Auclair (2012) have synthesized some of these as follows. They highlight that:

- Traditional indigenous water management techniques demonstrate an intimate knowledge of the natural environment and of different types of arid natural environments, of their surface and groundwater, of types of rain and wind. This resulted in the development of pragmatic approaches and water "technologies" that are focused on the detailed specificities of a place.
- They are also well adapted to a variety of water stakeholders and take account of both their needs and of the possibilities of water usage competition. For Moroccan sociologist Fatima Mernissi (1997), the capacity of Berber communities to manage their conflicts emerges from their very solid *social capital*. She explained that people such as the Berbers who have trust (*tiqa*), the capacity, and will to cooperate (*ta'awun*), who feel solidarity for each other (*tadamum*) and are capable of showing "unconditional tenderness" (*hannan*), can only have a very strong social capital. Mernissi also explored Berber tribal democratic principles within which collective and individual rights are equally defended.
- Finally, authors agree that most of the ingenious water management systems that best suited natural environment and communities were never born out of large-scale projects, nor from strongly centralized political systems (Pérennès, 1993: 77). They were limited to small scale, but their output was high.

As Pascon concluded, "*the role of traditional water management systems went well beyond water: in semi-arid regions where water could be a highly disputable resource, these systems illustrated a general mode of functioning in a society*" (in Pérennès, 1993: 19).

Nowadays, such participatory, communal management systems, recognized for their valorization of local know-how and their focus on sustainable development and environmental protection, are being rediscovered and reexplored. They are essentially revealed through the concept of "Agdal", described by Auclair (2012) as an "*anthropological curiosity, a communal management practice forgotten by developers and researchers, a local know-how progressively constructed and built on by generations of agro-pastors, an important part of the Moroccan Amazigh heritage, but also a socio-ecological concept with universal heuristic value"* (p. 23).

As a communal management system practiced in tribal societies where power was ill-defined, the *agdal* is a very old practice shared by a whole set of Berber people in North Africa and the Sahara. Rock engravings were found in the Atlas mountains of Morocco that illustrate the concept in ancient Amazigh pastoral communities (Auclair, 2012: 36). Since the concept encompasses the idea of luxuriant peaceful greenery, it merged with the notion of Islamic garden and was fully adopted by the Almoravid, Almohad, and Maranid dynasties who, as we previously saw, developed their own "city-agdals".

Auclair (2012) thoroughly studied the *Agdal* and explains that this term, which in Berber refers to the meadows and pasture in large areas of North Africa, is both a collective natural resource management technique, the specific territory within which this technique is being practiced, the laws of a specific community that are being applied, and a period of time indicating the alternance of opening and closing of this territory for pasture (p. 27). As Faouzi (2011) observed, the period of Agdal is publically announced in the souk.

To the question "what does the *agdal* represent to you?", asked to Berber communities during an enquiry in the High Atlas, one same answer was always given: "The Agdal represents the security of the tribe". For Berkes (2004), this illustrates well to what extent the agdal contributes to building resilience. Its rules are based on local know-how, designed and put into practice by users themselves. Its system of flexible management accounts for new experience, learning, and socio-ecological auto-feedback. It encourages a use of complementary natural resources that supports means of subsistence and minimizes risks.

The *agdal* expresses the link between two value systems that are fundamental in Amazigh rural society: honour, which controls exchanges and relationships between communities, and the *baraka* which controls humans–god links through the intermediary of saints. Some religious movements initiated the creation of great pastoral *agdals* in Morocco in the XVIIth c., in a context of extreme resources penury and generalized insecurity (Auclair, 2012: 35; Pascon, 1977).

Conclusion

In this chapter, we reviewed the mixed heritage that contributed to the design and build up of more and more refined water management techniques. What we now refer to as North African "traditional indigenous water management systems" benefited from techniques developed as far in the Antiquity. El Faiz (2015) explains that if people such as Abdel Aziz Belal, just as Morocco was becoming independent in 1956, considered that one essential task for the country was to integrate the core heritage of know-how within a strategy based on development and civilization, institutions did not, in fact, find appropriate ways to integrate the agricultural heritage into an economic emancipation that would also be respectful of sociocultural aspects.

In Part II, we explore how this detachment, and sometimes despise, for the water heritage of the country progressively gained importance, in the name of economic success and modernity.

References

Aguilar, B., L. Dispasquale and S. Mecca (2014) The patio house in Morocco: a sustainable design strategy. In Correia, M., Carlos, G., & Rocha S. (Eds.) *Vernacular Heritage and Earthen Architecture: Contributions for Sustainable Development*. London: Taylor and Francis.

Al Khalili, J. (2010) *Path Finders; The Golden Age of Arabic Science*. London: Penguin Books.

Auclair, L. and M. Alifriqui (2012) *Agdal. Patrimoine socio-écologique de l'Atlas marocain.* Publications de l'Institut Royal de la Culture Amazighe, Centre des Etudes Historiques et Environnementales, Série: Colloques et séminaires no. 29.

Azar, S. (2000) *Les sciences dans le monde arabe.* Paris: La croisée des chemins.

Benchaâbane, A. (2014) *Marrakech Cité-jardin. Grandeur, Décadence & Renaissance. Entretiens avec Laurence Gourret-Lapeyre.* Marrakesh: Borkane.

Berkes, F. (2004) Rethinking community-based conservation. *Conservation Biology.* 18 (3): 621–630.

El Faiz, M. (2015) *Agronomie et agronomes d'Al Andalous (XI –XIVe s.).* Casablanca: La croisée des chemins.

Faouzi, H. (2011) L'Agdal dans la dynamique des systèmes agraires des arganeraies des Haha. *Études Caribéennes* 20. http://journals.openedition. org/etudescaribeennes/5569, accessed 25th of June 2020.

Faruqui, N.I., A.K. Biswas and M.J. Bino (Eds.) (2001) *Water Management in Islam.* Tokyo, New York, Paris: United Nations University Press.

Lightfoot, D.R. (1996) Moroccan khetarras: traditional irrigation and progressive desiccation. *Geoforum.* 27 (2): 261–273.

Mernissi, F. (1997) *Les Ait Débrouille du Haut Atlas.* Casablanca: Le Fénnec.

Michel, G. (2016) *Les conférences des amis de Fès (1932–1956);* Tome 1. Iggybook.com

Panetier, J.L. and H. Limane (2002) *Volubilis, une cité du Maroc antique.* Paris: Ed. Maisonneuve et Larose/Malika. https://sitevolubilis.com/les-monuments-de-leau-2/ accessed on 7th of September 2020.

Pascon, P. (1977) *Le Haouz de Marrakech.* Rabat: Maisonneuve et Larose.

Pérennès, J. (1993) *L'eau et les hommes au Maghreb. Contribution à une politique de l'eau en Méditerranée.* Paris: Karthala.

Privitera, F. and Métalsi, M. (2016) *Le signe de la Médina. La morphologie urbaine selon Roberto Berardi.* Firenze: Dida Press.

Secret, E. (1990) *Les sept printemps de Fès,* Amiens.

Serrhini, F. (2003) L'eau à Fès, symbole d'une civilisation urbaine. *Revue H.T.E.,* No.26.

Sibley, M. (2006) The historic hammams of Damascus and Fès: lessons of sustainability and future developments. 23rd Conference on Passive and Low Energy Architecture, Geneva, Switzerland, 6–8 September 2006.

Tazi Sadeq, H. (2006) *Du droit de l'eau au droit à l'eau au Maroc et ailleurs.* Casablanca: La croisée des chemins.

Terrasse, H. (1954) Trois bains Mérénides. In Marcais, W. (Ed.) Mélanges, Paris.

Viviers, D. (2017) L'eau dans l'espace antique; le sacré, le pouvoir et la ville. In Fondation Esprit de Fès (Ed.) *Forum 2017: L'eau et le sacré. Fès.*

Watson, A.D. (1974) The Arab agricultural revolution and its diffusion, 700–1100. *Journal of Economic History.* 34 (1): 8–35.

Wolf, A. (2000) Indigenous approaches to water conflict resolution and implications for international waters. *International Negotiations, a Journal of Theory and Practice.* 5 (2): 357–373. www.transboundarywaters.orst.edu/publications/indigenous/ accessed 8th of October 2020.

Ziyad, A. (2017) La gestion de l'eau au Maroc à travers le temps, dans Fondation Esprit de Fès (Ed.) *Forum 2017: L'eau et le sacré. Fès.*

Part II

Paradigm shift

Characteristics of "modern water management" in Morocco

Introduction

Through a historical perspective, Part II illustrates how a version of modernity, a certain way of managing natural resources – especially land and water – emerged in Morocco that progressively detached human communities from their ecological milieu, and split communities, marginalizing and impoverishing many. While Part II illustrates what modernization meant in the context of Morocco, we feel it is worth reflecting first on the meaning of modernization, especially in relation to that of development.

Peng (2009), who thoroughly explored Luo Rongqu's book "A New Thesis on Modernization", concluded that scholars classified the meaning of modernization into four categories:

> 1. Modernization as a historical process by which economically 'slow' countries catch up with the world's more advanced countries through technological revolutions under the framework of specific international relations and modern capitalism. 2. Modernization, in essence, as industrialization. 3. Modernization as the process and the generalized categorization of the sudden and abrupt changes of humankind since the revolution in natural sciences. 4. Modernization as a set of changes in psychological attitudes, social values, and lifestyles.
>
> (p. 38)

Processes of modernization started as early as during the XIXth c. when, boosted by the industrial revolution, the economy of Europe developed steadily and a number of nation states were created. At the time:

> the Western world was widely perceived to be at the highest developmental stage of human social evolution. The social Darwinist

thought as well as biological rules of competition and survival of the fittest were seen everywhere. The aggressive momentum of capitalistic industrialization gave rise to an exciting and alluring feel of optimism, and it was believed that the non-Western world would use the Western world as an example to pursue "Westernization".

(Peng, 2009: 39)

In Morocco, processes of modernization started then, with the birth of a type of land management based on agrarian capitalism principles. Putting these in a historical context is key to help us understand how water management actors and water usage objectives changed and built the new premises for a modern water management system in the country.

The modernization phase that started after WWII and after the independence of the country (1956) added further complexity. After the traumas of the wars and economic depressions between the wars, a new sense of optimism had risen and *"the new claim by Western people after World War II that the Western model was the goal for development in the non-Western world became natural and beyond question"* (Peng, 2009: 39). For many, these optimistic claims were more specifically American than "Western" – only the United States had come out victorious of WWII and not suffered any cost. As a consequence, with Western theories of modernization having originated from America, the concept of modernization can really be better understood as, mainly, an American concept. In the context of decolonization, becoming a modern independent state – for a country such as Morocco – therefore carried a certain ethos. As Cooper puts it:

applied to Africa, the romance of modernization reflected the idea that America's restless urge to remake itself would rub off on a continent previously held by Europeans and which was just beginning to open itself to participation in an interactive world.

(2004: 27)

However, as Part II shows, this wave of optimism, related to novelty and modernization, also progressively absorbed the messages carried by the pan-Arabism movement. Now independent from France, and embracing the cause of other newly independent neighbouring North-African and Middle-Eastern countries, Morocco was free to not choose "the American way", in a rising cold-war climate and, instead, to unite with other Arab nations. However, with pro-Arabism not going necessarily hand in hand with pro-Berber, one of the objectives of the Berber movement had to be to assert the "Moroccanity" of Amazigh people and the importance of their culture at a time when Arabic culture was progressively being imposed on the country. Despite these efforts, one clear consequence of modernization was therefore the marginalization of all aspects of Berber culture, including the Berber approach to natural resources management. Like in India, where colonization had also occurred, development processes became increasingly associated with state authoritarianism, with a state-oriented notion of culture – the "state" being made up of institutions related to, influenced by, and dependent upon the international economy. Routledge (1987: 22, 23), who examined processes of development there as well as in many countries "from the South", stressed that:

> development has followed a path of capitalist industrialization that has concentrated employment, manufacturing and construction within cities and exacerbated rural poverty, leading to mass migration to urban areas. (…) This has been accompanied by an uneven cultural exchange that emphasizes Western values, equates modern scientific rationality and technology with a successful development process, and devalues non-modern indigenous cultures and their traditional systems of knowledge.

Describing development as a form of "Cultural Ethnocide" (Routledge 1987), the author went on criticizing water development initiatives such as the Narmada River Valley project, emphasizing that, in the context of such projects:

> local traditional cultures are viewed as impediments to progress and development. Whereas environmental costs are borne by the land, social and cultural costs are borne by the tribal communities. The unique ecology of specific regions - the symbiosis between nature and culture, environment and community - is irreparably damaged by the Juggernaut of modernization. In its wake, cultural disruption, social alienation and ethnic and economic marginalization prevail.

> (p. 23)

Originally "own" by the Protectorate administration, the concept of modernization and development progressively shifted to land in the hands of a newly independent country's government. As Cooper (2004: 22) – whose work focused on British and French decolonization – explained:

African political leaders in the 1950s turned developmentalist discourse in a direction favourable to them. For development to be in the interest of African people, they would argue, it was necessary for an African government to make the decisions about what development policy should be, for if not, there was danger that development would simply mean an escalation of exploitation.

Part II explores three aspects of the modernization process of the water management sector in Morocco and their shortcomings – technological modernization, economic modernization through market-centred strategies, and changes in governance. These three dimensions, observed through a historical perspective, describe how modern Morocco chose to "develop" – just before the Protectorate, then during the colonization period and then when it became independent – and how water, central to economic activities behind this development, got captured, mastered, priced, and ultimately overexploited. Whilst Part III will suggest alternative (post-modern) types of development and water management practices, Part II describes the breakdown of human–ecological links through a special take on modernity.

References

Cooper, F. (2004) Development, modernization and the social sciences in the era of decolonization: the examples of British and French Africa. *Revue d' Histoire des Sciences Humaines*. 1 (10): 9–38.

Peng, Y. (2009) Modernization theory. *Chinese Studies in History*. 43 (1): 37–45. doi: 10.2753/CSH0009-4633430104 accessed on 15th October 2020.

Routledge, P. (1987) Modernity as a vision of conquest: development and culture in India. In *Cultural Survival Quarterly Magazine*. www.culturalsurvival. org/publications/cultural-survival-quarterly/modernity-vision-conquest-development-and-culture-india, accessed on 23rd September 2020.

3 Modernizing water management

A historical perspective

The effects of the XIXth c. changes on water and land management

The XIXth c.: preamble to the French Protectorate

It is easy, in the spirit of post-colonialist studies, to point to the radical changes put in place during the Protectorate as the source of the country's difficulties in dealing with the current water crisis. Land management changes, the introduction of new agricultural practices, and the appropriation of water by some, indeed, did not help. However, in fairness, the form of agrarian capitalism that these were rooted in had already been put into place during the XIXth c. in Morocco. Although the Protectorate built on it, its new economic approaches had their specificities, as we will see later.

The various dimensions of the water crisis that Morocco is currently experiencing can find their origin during that past period. In particular, it is since then that the era of "the water of the State" has replaced the era of the "water of the sky".

The year 1830, with the arrival of France in Algeria, marks the beginning of long-lasting changes in Morocco's history. From then on, a chain of events cascaded, from which a sociopolitical and economic context emerged that was entirely favourable to the establishment of a Protectorate. As historians (Laroui, 1982; Pennell, 2003; Howe, 2005) have shown, the choice of the date that marks the start of the occupation of France in Algeria as a tipping point has both ideological political and economic *raison d'être*. When Algiers, then under Ottoman domination, was taken by the French in 1830, the geographical continuum of Dar Al-Islam, which had existed for 1000 years, was effectively broken: Morocco was no more linked to the Arab Middle East. Moroccan Moulay Abderrahmane, who wanted to rescue his Algerian

Muslim brothers, realizing that his army was disorganized and badly equipped, had decided to purchase weapons as well as training for his soldiers. *"This really marked the beginning of heated commercial rivalries among European powers who were keen to obtain mining concessions, trade advantages and influence in this unruly kingdom"* (Howe, 2005: 62). The mining potential (with reserves of copper and rock salt, in particular) was huge, but underexploited. If the Moroccan response to this was positive, that was mainly due to the Sultans' incapacity to raise enough money for their country solely through taxes permitted by the *shari'a* (Islamic law) – that is: the *zakat* on cattle and the *ushur* on harvests. Despite the strong disapproval of the *ulamas* (wise religious elders), Moulay Abderrahmane encouraged international trade, in particular through commercial activities carried out by powerful families (Benjelloun, Ben Idris, Bennis) as well as Jewish families who had always traded with Southern European partners. From the first half of the XIXth c., Morocco therefore started exporting cereals, whool, and wax. At the time, British traders were majoritarian as trading partners. A treaty gave Morocco commercial access to European products in 1956 (Pennell, 2003). Sultans became more and more dependent on the elite of powerful families who benefited directly from this trade. In the second half of the XIXth c., European traders who settled in Tangiers also multiplied corrupt commercial deals with their "Moroccan *protégés*", and trading activities lost a lot of their transparency.

Moulay Abderrahman, conscious that foreign money raised from commercial activities was being used by numerous local powerful people to consolidate their autonomy against the palace, in his turn, created alliances with powerful families (El Goundafi, El Glaoui, El Mtouggi – the "great *caiids*"). Both sides collided in 1894 (Pennell, 2003), when the sultan died. As Abdallah Laroui stressed, by then, the Moroccan State had already ceased to exist when, in 1880, the kingdom was placed under international control at the Conference of Madrid. Soon later, in 1906, the opening of Morocco to international trade culminated with the Algeciras Pact, which gave economic equality to all European powers at stake. The massive import of European products, however, rapidly killed embryonic local industries and led to the devaluation of the national currency.

Political domination was given to France in Morocco, in exchange for Italian domination in Lybia, British domination over Egypt, and specific rights for Spain in the Western Sahara. Europeans and the US promised in the Algeciras Pact to ensure that order, peace, and prosperity would be maintained in Morocco.

Consequences for land and water management

How does this relate to water management? Through the transformation of agricultural practices and strategies, clearly. Why agriculture?
Because it requires water, and also land, whose management radically
changes, to a large extent, as a result of trade policies. Lazarev describes
this as the emergence of large state properties and of rent domains in
Morocco, prior to the Protectorate (2014: 81–122). The emergence of
this new type of agrarian capitalism violently changed a rural society
that was then dominated by modes of communal production (based on
small-scale agricultural production, cattle farming, and arts and crafts)
and, intermittently, on feudal types of agricultural production.

The main stakeholders behind such changes, for whom, from then
on, land property became the *new economic term of reference*, included:

- The entire ruling class, imperial family, traditional entourage of
  the sovereign, military chieves – in other words, the *"Makhzen"*.
  The land capital of these powerful families was however taken back
  from them if their political fortune collapsed. The land then had to
  be redistributed.
- The *bourgeois merchants* – mainly based in Fès, these people had
  privileged trading deals with Manchester or Marseille. They formed
  a new group of business people whose activities focused on land
  speculation; they really created the bases of agrarian capitalism in
  Morocco. It is ironic to notice that, despite the rural focus of their
  main new interest, these people were essentially urban citizens and
  knew very little about "their land".
- Another category of land owners had, during the XIXth c., put in
  place some feudal models of management of huge properties. The
  "lords" of such *Zawyias* saw in land ownership a way to strengthen
  their political power. To them, this was more attractive than cumu-
  lating wealth in a capitalist way.
- Finally, the intellectual *Chorfas*, the traditional aristocracy, also
  became seduced by land management and started enjoying the rent
  derived from their domains. They were allies to the sultan and were
  tax exempt.

At the end of the XIXth c., Moroccan land was thus far from united.
As Boukhari (2012) eloquently put it:

> whilst the industrial revolution was taking over the Western world at
> high speed, Morocco was jealously closing itself. (…) The political

anarchy in place made the old Empire look like a man on the verge of a nervous breakdown. The country was cut into two: the *bled Makhzen* (plains, ports, big cities), under the sultan's authority and the *bled siba* (the mountains), inhabited by the rebels. The borders between the two fluctuated with waves of punishing expeditions aimed at ensuring that people were paying their taxes.

The worsening of the situation regarding land management had therefore generated a context that would make the appropriation of land by the French colons very easy indeed. In the name of agrarian capitalism it had, even before the Protectorate, seriously damaged the pillars of traditional rural tribes who, for millennia, had been working hard at maintaining a socioecological and economic balance. This balance, which reflected the agronomic and water heritage acquired since the Antiquity, was about to be destroyed by civilizing missions and "development programs" introduced by the Protectorate. As Boukhari (2012) concludes:

> Morocco's misfortune lies in the fact that its decadence coincided with the emergence of a new ideology: colonialism. (…) Already way down, with its feet and hands tied up, the country saw the Protectorate that was imposed to it as the only way to "be saved".

How a radical shift in paradigm, under the Protectorate, sow the seeds for new water management practices

The French Protectorate: definition and impacts on water policies

From 1912 until 1956, Morocco experienced a particular type of colonization under the French Protectorate. A Protectorate is defined as a specific political regime, put into place via a Treaty, which specifies that a protecting State controls another, protected, State. Although Morocco signed the Treaty, its sultan, Moulay Abelhafid did so very reluctantly. He was forced to abdicate by Lyautey, first general resident of the French Protectorate in 1912, who replaced him with his son, Moulay Hassan – himself very badly accepted by most regions in Morocco – against financial compensation that allowed him to live very comfortably in Tangiers.

In total, the "colonial conquest" lasted for 25 years, with Moroccan people firmly showing their animosity against the French army through some famous battles (such as the Rif War 1921–1926, and the uprisings of Boufekrane in 1937). The names of true heroes (such as Mohamed ben Abdelkrim Et-Khattabi) remain engraved in the history of the country. In an attempt to calm the situation, the institutions of the Protectorate focused on three strategies:

1 First, gain the trust of powerful local regional personalities, as the Makhzen had previously done, in order to help maintain a certain order. The objective was for the Protectorate to be able to focus their efforts on regions they considered as more interesting economically.
2 Second, maintain what they thought constituted the traditional structure of society: that is, a division between Arab and Berber communities. French people were interested in the fact that Berbers had a non-Islamic legal system and were attached to the land in a way that could make them good allies for French settlers. Incorporating them within the French Protectorate's agenda would take them away from nationalist Islamist and Arab ideals. The French institutions therefore put into place a legal system that could deal with the Berber customary laws by creating a Dahir (treaty), in 1914.
3 Third, put strong emphasis on the fact that the Sultan remained the sovereign of his country, that new laws would be promulgated in his name, and that the structure of the Makhzen was to be kept in place, with the Great Vizir leading it, and the Moroccan flag as a national emblem.

As for the protective characteristic of the Protectorate, it remains debatable. Montligeon (1932: 299) explains that Article 5 of the Protectorate Treaty focused on the exclusive right of France to talk to Foreign powers on behalf of the sultan and his government. However, whilst the sultan prescribed legal matters, it was down to the resident general to have the exclusive power to make them applicable. Article 1 expressed France's commitment to maintain the internal sovereignty of the sultan, the maintenance of the religious situation and the respect and prestige of the sultan. France, however, had the right to control each act of sovereignty of the sultan. The concept of "protection" was therefore mainly translated through strong recommendations as to how to manage internal affairs, as well as how to structure the action of various types of stakeholders, throughout a territory whose geographical and ethnic specificities were never taken into consideration by the colonial authorities. By the time Mohamed V took power in 1927, recommendations made by the colonial authorities were considered in a much less "docile" way. That period, described as the "revolution of the King and his people", led to the exile of S.M. Mohamed V in 1953 and was disturbed by numerous Resistance attacks, strikes, and military interventions by the Moroccan Liberation Army. Ultimately, this led to the independence of the country, in 1956.

For now, what is of interest to us is the impact that this way of managing a country had in the area of water resources. With regard to these, the Protectorate is characterized by quite radical actions in terms of economic strategies, major changes in agricultural modes of production, administrative divisions of the land and of communities and, more generally, by the introduction of a new economic paradigm, entirely foreign to Moroccan people and authorities, and badly understood nor integrated, from the very start.

The complexity of changes generated in water management under the Protectorate are closely linked to changes observed in land management.

Prior to the Protectorate, rural communities were used to making decisions and managing changes locally and independently from Higher Authority. As Mohammed Naciri from the Agronomy and Veterinary Institute Hassan II of Rabat explains, at the time:

> all initiatives related to land management were out of the central power's reach: the intervention of the State in local economic life was extremely reduced if not totally absent. The relationship with local regions was merely based on political allegiance. The central authority, the Makhzen, was therefore never equipped to make decisions related to local communities; its level of intervention was the whole territory of Morocco.
>
> (Naciri, 1985: 228)

Consequently, local communities resisted against the central management of their resources. Any new initiative would lead to the mobilization and involvement of the local population as well as strategic negotiations with the central power.

Clearly, things changed when rural communities were, for the first time in the history of their country, submitted to centralized ruling under the Protectorate, in 1934. The French administration chose to impose itself on the rural world by managing conflicts between tribes. Its objective was to transform the mountain communities into allies against nationalist movements that were growing in cities, and that were threatening to expand into the plains and the rich agricultural areas that it needed. However:

> the consequences of these changes were numerous. Pastoral nomadic movements, ecological foundation of tribal autonomy, were upset, and the whole organisation of the terroir was disturbed.

The arbitrage set in terms of land, pasture and water, sealed the inbalances created amongst communities.

(Naciri, 1985: 228)

The administrative division of land and the breakdown of communities

Right at the beginning of the Protectorate, under the Lyautey administration (1912–1922), strategic decisions were made to economically develop the country. A certain number of factors were considered as key to future prosperity since they would help reaching budgetary equilibrium. One of them was to colonize land, another was the development of industries, whilst the third was the exploitation of underground resources, such as the newly discovered phosphate. These were part of a broader "modernization package" aiming to use important investments but which was badly perceived or integrated in the rural world which, so far, had not been modernized at all.

In addition to being dependent on the acquisition of the land, the training of labourers and putting into place a good irrigation system, the strategy of "valorization of the land" implied a new ingenious legal system, a clever use of funds but, above all, the settlement of "colons". This would itself generate an entirely new social environment.

Before being able to operationalize this strategy, the French institutions had to find a way of acquiring land. The way to do so, ingenious for the colons, insidious for the others, focused on various legal manipulations of Dahirs (treaties) that would allow the Protectorate to manage certain pieces of land – the most fertile ones. The starting point was to draw a classification of land status, which revealed that the following different types of land existed at the beginning of the XXth c.:

* The "dead land", without "master", were considered as available goods. However, they were generally sterile and extremely difficult to cultivate. In Muslim law, whoever manages to vivify this land becomes its owner.
* Private land had (and still have) rights defined by the *Jmaa*. The 1924 Dahir regulated civil justice in terms of recognition and transmission of such property.
* *Habbou land* (belonging to religious foundations) had been mobilized by the sovereign for religious reasons: they could not be transmitted but could therefore not be colonized either. The French Protectorate suggested they could become "private properties" – and this allowed them to purchase them.

- Collective property included land that belonged to a socioethnic group. Somebody inheriting from a particular individual could not have access to a collective piece of land. This collective land included both land that could be cultivated and pasture land for cattle farmers and nomads. No document, at the time, existed that would guaranty the status of such property, carefully looked after by tribes. At the time, collective property could only be "alienated" if it allowed the State to make a profit for the public good. This is how this land could be mobilized for official colonization under the Protectorate.

- The *Makhzen land*, the biggest one and most accessible, belonged to the State. The principles of public domains allowed everybody to use it, and no one in particular to own it. It also included the private domain of the sultan. Legally speaking, the *Makhzen land* belonged to the Muslim community. Legally speaking, they were not to be sold – and only their usufruct could be conceded by the sovereign, in his quality of *imâm*. The French Protectorate encouraged the changes in status of parts of this land. Some other types of land, which could therefore be sold to the French, had previously belonged to personalities who had later fallen into disgrace. In some other rather extreme cases, some of these pieces of land were even sold at auctions – even though, traditionally, they had always been considered as inalienable.

French institutions also found ways to buy most of what previously belonged to owners living in cities. Besides, the creation of personal domains was done through the purchase of pieces of land previously own by farmers struck by poverty, droughts, and financial difficulties.

As Lazarev explains:

> since the appropriation of land by foreigners was forbidden, fructuous deals with Moroccan owners were made: those pretended to own pieces of land that were in fact owned by tribal collectivities. The spoliation was encouraged by numerous instances of abuse of power which could be seen in areas where influential families of the Makhzen had settled.
>
> (2014: 121)

Twists to existing legal arrangements were imagined, animated by the French anxiety of having a Protectorate without land or colons. Consequently, the next effort of the colonial administration was to find ways of attracting people to Morocco and for them to settle in this new country.

At the time, some considered that Morocco was ill-adapted to a model of "grand colonization", based on large-scale agricultural land. However, certain powerful French companies had taken investment risks with political objectives in mind – ensuring that the colonization in Morocco would remain in the hands of the French and that German interests would be dissuaded. Consequently, the "great colonization" model was kept and focused on making the coast productive by building ports on the one hand, and on growing certain agricultural products (olive, oranges...) for exports on the other. French people were encouraged to settle through incentive schemes (including 10–12 years credits for the payment of their land; subsidies for monoculture, 50% exemption of land taxes, and total tax exemption on difficult pieces lands that people would be prepared to valorize themselves).

The first wave of colons arrived in 1914. The second in 1920. Initially, people settled in the Chaouia and the Doukkala plains, then in the area of Marrakech, then in Fès and Tadla. As a whole, it is the Casa-Rabat-Kénitra area which attracted most people. Lyautey saw the ideal "colon" as a "gentleman farmer" – not as a hard-working small-scale farmer. This probably contributed to the fact that 4/5th of the 379,000 hectares occupied by the French in 1922 were of average size ("moyenne colonization") and that the remaining 1/5th corresponded to the "grande colonization", managed by the great companies. No farm was small. The surface of the fields justified the use of modern equipment. Farms were big enough for families to settle, and for their children to be able to carry on cultivating the land without having to go and find work elsewhere. Progressively, the colons worked on bigger farms. They focused on the most fertile land and on export crops.

What is for sure is that the new legal arrangements put into place by the Protectorate administration, as well as the division of agricultural land that resulted from it, led to the breakdown of rural communities and generated important inequalities.

Renowned for doing exactly that was the Berber Dahir of 1930, which contributed to the separation of Berber mountains communities from Arab urban dwellers from the plains. The Arabs were under civilian control. The Berbers, on the other hand, were respecting customary law and under military command. Not being submitted to Coranic law, the Berbers were therefore only dependent on French tribunals and custom jurisdiction ("*orf*"). The Protectorate saw in this Dahir a possibility to create alliances with the Berbers, which would help them create a counterweight to the rising importance of the Arab nationalist movement in the cities and in the plains.

"This marginalisation of the mountain, in view of benefiting the plain by giving it access to water, as well as the creation of a 'useful, productive Morocco' opposed to a 'useless, unproductive' one, contributed to generating a massive migration towards cities and a rapid urban growth. This phenomenon broke the structure of the Moroccan society and encouraged the creation of nationalist movements" (instead of dissuading them).

(El Jihad, 2001: 266)

From the point of view of water management, the enhancement of agricultural land quite rapidly resulted in the capture of water resources for the benefit of an economy based on export crops and ignorant of the need for community equity or ecological equilibrium in an arid environment. One of the illustrative examples of such approach exists in the Targa area, just outside Marrakesh. As Benchaâbane explains:

the orchards that European colons created in Targa allowed them to produce citrus products targeted for the French market. At the end of last century, water shortages were observed in all of these orchards following droughts that had lowered down the level of the water table in that region. In Targa, the water table has been well over-exploited. Electric pumps put into place by farmers ended up exhausting water reserves that were completely dried up in less than a century.

(2014: 64)

Therefore, if geographical and socioeconomical inequalities rose during the Protectorate, inequalities also emerged from the uneven access to water that resulted from agricultural practices encouraged during that period. The next section focuses more specifically on changes in ways of approaching water management.

The influence of the Protectorate on changes in the water paradigm

Beyond the division of land and the destructuration of rural communities, the economic strategies of the Protectorate had important repercussions on what could be described as a "water paradigm" – i.e., a way of approaching water issues.

In the first place, "water from the sky", considered as a gift from God in Islam that needs to be managed, shared, and given following very specific traditional codes of conduct, ended up becoming "water from the State" (Pascon, 1978), suddenly manipulated and dominated by new laws and legal amendments imposed by the French Protectorate. Directly behind it, and giving their blessing to these rather radical changes, were groups of powerful Moroccan people associated to the Makhzen and involved in the actions undertaken by colonial forces. The principles and codes of "good water management" that had been put into place by previous rules were being got rid of. The imposition of new rules disturbed not only the physical water management but also the relationship between water stakeholders.

Secondly, water usage, which, in terms of volume, had been kept moderate by both farmers and nomadic communities, had so far respected a socioecological logic. Most often, agriculture production followed a rather modest type of subsistence agriculture that was not connected to a market type of economy. Water usage responded to a survival logic rather than a logic based on generating monetary wealth. The Protectorate introduced a paradigm focused on modern economics and export agriculture, which inevitably led people to perceive water issues in a radically different way. From being considered as a rare and even sacred natural resource, it abruptly became a mere ingredient, an economic factor, whose quantity and means of use were to be allocated for the purpose of optimizing the production of economic goods.

Thirdly, the shift in water paradigm affected the way in which people perceived the land and the territory. Moroccan tribes had learnt, throughout centuries, to live with water scarcity in arid or semi-arid regions, as well as to deal with climate changes that would make periods of abundance alternate with moments of penury. They knew how to adapt to varied natural environments, such as mountains and plains, or places with very irregular relief, as well as how to negotiate and live with various types of human communities, sedentary, or nomads. The main distinction that the Protectorate focused on was the one between the "useful Morocco" and the "unproductive – useless – one". Rarely, throughout retrospective analyses of the regions having been colonized in the world, can we find more despising expressions than this one, invented by people whose role was to be "protect" and "develop" and who had – some would even dare say – a "civilizing mission".

Legal changes related to land

We will first explore how, from a situation in which the Protectorate administration feared to not have enough land to work on and to produce from, it moved to another quite different one where it possessed the most fertile land in the country.

As Benali (2006: 76) stressed:

> even prior to the achievement of any water infrastructure, the colonial power initiated a policy change aimed at giving water resources a modern legal status. Coranic law and customary laws were seen as being insufficiently precise (...) and the French legislation was therefore used to constitute the "Moroccan Water Code". In this way, water resources could be integrated into the public sphere through an "elegant domanial solution" which, subsequently, allowed the colonial State to monopolise and to control water resources.

This would later be followed by the creation of measures concerning the land. As early as in 1913, The Dahir on land status registering provided the legal bases and practical modalities for land acquisition. On a regular basis, and until 1951, a phenomenal amount of work focused on the creation of a legal arsenal that would focus on land management and would help colonial forces to settle further. These texts reminded that collective property was recognized as belonging to tribes and that the *Jmaa* (legal wise elders of the villages) was expected to deal with matters related to changes in land management and ownership. However, the *Jmaa* was also obliged to be assisted by the Direction of Indigenous Affairs and by the Cherifian Council (who were both controlled by the authorities of the Protectorate) when making decisions. Needless to say, the "assistance" could have a big influence on the final decision. Although collective pieces of land belonging to the tribe were unseizable and imprescriptible, the community was allowed to let its land – it however could not dispose of it. However the tribe had the right, albeit with the correct authorization to do so, to carry out a share of the land "by tent" – that is, to divide the property amongst all the members that made up "the collectivity". This operation could be carried out once each member had revivified the part of the collective land that had been let to him. As Montligeon (1932) observed, it is therefore through this ingenious method, which is precisely conform to Muslim laws and customs, that the French Protectorate managed to mobilize very large parts of the Moroccan territory (1932: 191). Consequently, already in 1913, that is, one year after the establishment of the Protectorate, French settlers already possessed land that had been acquired thanks to valid legal processes.

In terms of land ownership, radical changes were therefore happening. That process, however, was reminiscent of another one that had led to the creation of "*domaines de rente*" at the beginning of the XIXth c., when agrarian capitalism emerged. Traditionally, rural Moroccan society was dominated by a communal mode of production or, as was the case in certain regions in very intermittent ways, by a feudal type of production. During the XIXth c. (it started in the rural areas between Fès and Tangiers and in the periphery of ports), this mode of production was, for the first time, transformed into a system based on "rent". This was an important transformation in the Moroccan society because it hit the core of society, Fès and the Makhzen, and was one of the main factors that led to the creation of the contemporary Fassi bourgeoisie. The agrarian type of capitalism created by the Protectorate was not entirely similar to the initial model: it therefore grew as a competing model to the initial one, born in the XIXth c., and that was just starting to consolidate. Lazarev (2014) explored how the Protectorate administration managed to question the non-alienability of pieces of land that belonged to families related to the sultan, to civil servants from the traditional Makhzen, and even from chieves. Through their interpretation of Muslim law, the protectorate powers managed to make such transfers unequivocally official.

Most of the capitalist social group that had started to emerge did not disappear: not only didn't it lose its advantages, but the Protectorate ensured that it could benefit even more from the colonial system by developing its business and expanding the land capital it had acquired prior to 1912.

Legal changes related to water

Water policies put into place by the French Protectorate, far from being focused on technological and agricultural changes, were first of a legal nature. Legal changes were necessary for colonizing forces to be able to establish themselves. The numerous and varied legal experiences that the French had acquired in Algeria and Tunisia were finely adapted to the Moroccan context. It is however in this country that the existing legal system in place was the hardest to manipulate. Customary laws related to water were as varied as perennial, and certainly not unified.

For these reasons, the colonial administration had to create numerous exceptions, officialized by the Dahir of July 1925 (articles 10 and 11). The most solid and politically acceptable solution was to integrate water resources into the public domain. The Protectorate succeeded in doing so through the Dahir of July 1914, modified in 1919. In both texts, the law integrated rivers and groundwater into the public domain. Legal professionals and, in particular, Mr Sonnier (author of the 1935 Water

Code), had attempted to justify the principle of domaniality using Muslim law as their premise. They explained that:

> in Islam, water was, in principle, a good that was aimed to benefit all (right of *"chirb"* and right of *"chafa"*) and which required special authorisation from the sovereign himself if it was to become private. The colonial conquest was unable to deny this type of principle, which corresponds to our principle of domaniality of public water.
>
> (Sonnier, 1933: 48)

For Pérennès (1993: 121), asserting that water was part of the public domain and accompanying this assertion with the recognition of traditional rights that existed prior to 1914 *"was, in fact, a subtle way to stop these from evolving whilst, at the same time, sounding virtuous for respecting people's rights – albeit, in a rather cheap fashion"*. By putting new acquisitions under the control of the State, Lyautey's policy found ways to protect the interests of both local chieves and colonial institutions. Since water from the public domain was available to users, and not to owners, it meant that the Administration was keen to maintain social order by avoiding all that would jeopardize the coexistence of Moroccan and colonial interests. The colonization largely benefited from these arrangements.

Conclusion

This chapter illustrated how indigenous practices that have evolved for centuries – based on the careful study of the natural environment and of how communities interact with it – can be very rapidly disrupted by radical shifts. These shifts can be physical, technological, or affecting the way in which land is being distributed and worked on. It was the case in Morocco when the French Protectorate introduced new economic objectives as well as new ways of thinking and governing.

While it is easy to assume that such changes only appeared under the Protectorate, with the establishment of a rather forceful French administration – despite its "protective" mission, they can in fact be quite well synthesized in the notion of "agrarian capitalism". This concept, which had already appeared in the XIXth c., reinforced new administrative divisions of land and introduced radically different ways of understanding what "looking after the land" means, and for whom.

When the Protectorate was established, land acquisition and division carried on, with a few variations and evolutions from those initiated during the previous century. Altogether, however, these land management changes had very strong implications for the management of water since both types of resources are strongly linked, especially through Muslim laws. The radical legal modifications that were generated by the French Protectorate justified European actions and very much confused some others. In total, not only land and water resources changed status but, more importantly, Moroccan communities were broken up. In particular, and despite the fact that the Berber Dahir had been rejected by the majority of people who saw Berbers and Arabs as linked in their "Moroccanity", communities from the mountains were marginalized and impoverished against the plains and cities, occupied by the Arabs and the Europeans. Whilst legal arrangements contributed to this impoverishment, the next chapter explains how the modernization of economics, technologies, and governance of water resources, also did – and carry on to do so.

References

Benali, A. (2006) *Aménagement étatique, gestion sociale de l'eau et dynamiques institutionnelles de la PMH au Maroc.* Louvain: Presses Universitaires de Louvain.

Benchaâbane, A. (2014) *Marrakech Cité-jardin. Grandeur, Décadence & Renaissance. Entretiens avec Laurence Gourret-Lapeyre.* Marrakesh: Borkane.

Boukhari, K. (2012) Comment le Maroc a été vendu avant le Protectorat. *SlateAfrique* www.slateafrique.com/92955/histoire-comment-le-maroc-ete-vendu, accessed on 11th of September 2020.

El Jihad, M. Moulay Driss (2001) L'eau de la montagne et le pouvoir étatique au Maroc; entre le passé et le présent. *Annales de géographie.* 110 (622): 665–672.

Howe, M. (2005) *Morocco. The Islamist Awakening and Other Challenges.* Oxford: Oxford University Press.

Laroui, A. (1982) *L'histoire du Maghreb: un essai de synthèse*, 2 volumes (2nd Ed.). Paris: Maspero.

Lazarev, G. (2014) Ruralité et changement social. Etudes sociologiques. Université Mohamed V Agdal. *Publications de la Faculté des Lettres et Sciences Humaines Rabat. Série Essais et Etudes* N. 64. Rabat: Edition et Impressions Bouregreg.

Montligeon sous la direction de Albert de Pouvourville (1932) *Histoire populaire des colonies françaises – le Maroc.* Paris: Editions du Velin d'or.

Naciri, M. (1985) L'aménagement de l'espace territorial au Maroc. Lieux d'autonomie et centralisation étatique. *Annuaire de l'Afrique du nord. Rubrique Etudes.* 18 pages. http://aan.mmsh.univ-aix.fr/Pdf/AAN-1983-22_21.pdf accessed on 03rd of November 2020.

Pascon, P. (1978) De l'eau du ciel a l'eau d'Etat. Psycho-sociologie de l'irrigation. *HTE.* (48): 3–10.

Pennell, C.R. (2003) *Morocco. From Empire to Independence.* Oxford: Oneworld Book.

Pérennès, J. (1993) *L'eau et les hommes au Maghreb. Contribution à une politique de l'eau en Méditerranée.* Paris: Karthala.

Sonnier, A. (1933) *Le régime juridique des eaux au Maroc.* Rabat: Institut des Hautes Etudes marocaines.

4 Three key characteristics of Moroccan water management in the XXth c.

Modernity and technology

The focus on dams

At the end of the Protectorate, the Moroccan economy, considered as underdeveloped, was dominated by agricultural activities. These were split into a traditional, not very productive, sector, and a modern one represented by one million hectares of colonized land. These activities were aimed at improving the food security of a fast-growing population and at increasing the economic wealth through exportation: it contributed to one-third of the GNP.

Agriculturally focused activities had been initiated under the Protectorate, which was already very keen to export products such as citrus fruits, tomatoes, and beetroot to France. To do so, it had boosted large-scale production and had completely transformed the way in which water resources were managed and distributed. However, the initial choice for the *"Grande Hydraulique"* had been controversial, opposing civil engineers to geographers and agronomists who had worked in Algeria and Tunisia. Very keen to draw lessons from their experiences, these specialists had highlighted the numerous (socioeconomic and ecological) problems generated by the construction of large dams. A minority of engineers, such as Jean Coignet, defended a small-scale water management approach. Although they were backed up by researchers such as Arrus (in Pérennès, 1993: 126), who denounced big French construction firms and banks for using Morocco as an experimental field for building dams and exporting their capital, advocates of small-scale irrigation and subsistence agriculture lost the battle.

From being a horizontal type of management before the Protectorate, water management went almost entirely "vertical", with the State becoming the main decision-maker for the entire country. Some described this historical threshold (Jouve, 2006; El Faiz, 2000) as "*the transformation of the era of the water from the sky into that of the State's water*". The "triumphant State" based its strategy on the powerful technological ethos behind the "*politique des barrages et de la Grande Hydraulique*". Whilst 13 small dams had been built by the French by 1956, King Hassan II, through large-scale water projects and the construction of large dams, dreamt of transforming his country into the California of Africa by focusing on the generation of hydroelectricity and on an important capacity to irrigate extensive agricultural units.

Relying on technological "grandeur" to assert the strength of newly independent countries was not new: the Egyptian State had done the same when building the Aswan dam. It had even commissioned artists to compose nationalist songs in favour of the dam (Al Sadd al-Ali had thus been written and sang by the popular singer Abd al Halim Hafiz) (Reynolds in Mikhail, 2013). Marthelot (1961) similarly highlighted the fact that Moroccan dams are often called after old sovereigns or famous historical battles. For Troin (in Ihazrir, 2009: 619), this could also reflect an attempt to integrate rural roots into modern development.

Between 1970 and 1979, one dam was built each year. Seven out of these nine were large dams, with a total capacity of more than 7 billion m^3. Six of the nine were designed to irrigate a total of 326,000 hectares. During the last three decades of the XXth c., between 43% and 77% of investments therefore focused on agriculture, with 50% of public investments, between 1965 and 1983, being entirely kept to finance the construction of dams (corresponding to 243 million dollars) (Krouz, 1992). In the following years, dams captured 50% of agricultural investments.

Definitely putting aside the "intervention from the sky", the Moroccan State, during those years, therefore put into place the very ambitious plan to irrigate a million hectares. That objective was reached in 1997 and, that same year, the El Wahda dam was inaugurated: it was the second largest dam in the whole of Africa.

The reliance on technology in general, and dams, in particular, carried on being seen as a good environmental and economic option, even through the 1980s – a long period of droughts. Then, building small and average size dams started being envisaged as a way of creating jobs in the rural world in addition to capturing water.

Over the long-run, in Morocco, the social dimensions resulting from the construction of large dams have mostly been negative. Local communities never adhered to the large dam projects. From a technical perspective, these did not correspond to their way of technically approaching water management. When they were asked to contribute by helping reforest the areas surrounding the dams, they refused to do so as a sign of protest against the new water tariffs that had been imposed to them and the unfavourable financial conditions of new water credits in place. The State's strategy, based on modern technologies, could not last in the long-run if the population were not involved in the adoption and appropriation of these techniques or, even worse, if they were deprived from the benefits that these technological advances were supposed to bring to the country. This however is what happened.

The construction of new dams is still part of the water agenda of Morocco. Twelve (12) large dams and 26 small dams are currently being built (El Ghomari, 2015). However, new ways of controlling the amount of water needed for human and economic needs must be rethought. As Imad Boulahat stressed in an interview with Economie Entreprises (2020), building dams is no use if they do not fill for lack of rain or if, as it is the case, the evaporation is such that it leads to huge water loss. Besides, ecologically, there is a huge problem of siltation, generating the loss of 75 million m³ of water every year (L'Opinion, 2020). The objective is not only to increase water supply, but, more and more, to generate hydroelectricity. Doing so, – which would, as Doukali stressed, would save an average 70,000 tonnes of oil per year (Doukkali, 2005: 73). One can hope that the new Moroccan initiatives focused on renewable energy will highlight the existence of alternatives to that plan.

Irrigation techniques

The technological rationale behind the construction of dams was directly related to the will to irrigate more land and transform a large proportion of the country into industrial agricultural production units – based on extensive mechanized agriculture and export crops.

At the beginning of the 1960s, the *"Politique des barrages"* focused on the great Atlantic plains. These had already been "preselected" by the Protectoral authorities and had led to the division of irrigated land into various types. As a result, the Doukkala plain, for instance, received particular attention, with the construction of various dams between 1929 and 1937. The improvement of irrigation techniques in those parts of the country were such that, whilst in 1960, 4700 hectares were irrigated, 14,000 hectares were irrigated only 7 years later.

As a whole, policies focused on large-scale irrigation have been perceived as successful: they have generated economic wealth. However, farmers who were given the choice preferred to carry on cultivating pieces of land that were smaller than the recommended size. They chose to cultivate cereals and vegetables, which gave them more economic independence in an economic system traditionally dominated by a sub-sistence agricultural system (Krouz, 1992).

At the end of the XXth c., as Bennis and Tazi Sadeq (1998) explain, two main irrigation systems dominated: the "Grande Hydraulique" focused on very large-scale surfaces (500,000 hectares), thanks to dams from which water could be used all year long. A much more modest surface of the agricultural land relied on small- and medium-scale irri-gation, using unregulated water resources. The proportion of irrigated land increased considerably since the independence of the country – from 90,000 hectares in 1961 to 1,458,000 hectares in 2004 (HCP, 2007).

> The State's intention [was] to increase the surface of land that was continuously irrigated during the whole year to 60% of irrigated land so as to ensure the food security of the country. This objective could be reached thanks to the modernisation of agricultural equipment in certain regions.
>
> (Bennis and Sadeq, 1998: 8)

This approach, however, generated sociological and economic problems. The State created some Associations of Water Users, which they hoped would embrace the technological changes they had introduced. However, these were perceived as complex and modern and were neither understood nor favoured by farmers who were not keen to have to suffer additional annual costs to take part in agricultural pol-icies they had not agreed to. The costs based on water consumption, and the unit prices that had been set, clearly exceeded those that had been put in place regionally by customary laws. One of the main questions that the current Moroccan "Green Plan" focuses on therefore deals with finding the most appropriate ways in which the population should be involved when putting a sustainable development strategy into place. This is a fundamental question and an economic and sociopolitical one.

The State is progressively suggesting that *"Food security could also be reached by relying more on traditional irrigation systems based on cus-tomary law used to distribute water resources"* (Bennis and Tazi Sadeq, 1998: 8). Learning how to reintegrate traditional irrigation systems into current production system could therefore be one the main challenges.

From surface water to groundwater

One noticeable change in water management, derived from a mod-ernization of the sector, was related to a progressive shift from sur-face water usage to groundwater exploitation. Whilst some projects focused on capturing surface water, especially in mountainous areas

(1700 million m³ per year), a whole network of wells and projects of drilling always deeper aimed at capturing 4 billion m³ of water each year (MEMEE-DE, 2011). Since the independence of the country, surface water has been overexploited and the move to groundwater usage has been as rapid as ecologically destructive. The reliance on cheap technology provided by unregulated drilling companies was not stopped by the State, worried that farmers in need of financial revenue, would violently protest. As a consequence, water stress has considerably increased in Morocco and water tables have not been replenished in the way traditional water management systems previously ensured they did.

Water transfers

As is the case in many other parts of the world, water is naturally unequally distributed throughout Morocco and some areas are more water-rich than others. Transferring water from these to the most deprived areas is not new: indeed, the Almoravid dynasty had already used the Middle Eastern techniques of the khettaras to transport water from the mountains to the plains and this had indeed helped them create their capital city: Marrakesh. Water transfers using surface canals started under the Protectorate with the creation of the Canal de la Rocade. Piping (avoiding evaporation) has also been used to transfer water between different regions. The investments and reliance on technological advances allowing for these transfers have been considerable and carry on being envisaged as necessary. It is currently planned to transfer 800 million m³ water from the North to the South (El Ghomari, 2015).

In addition, other modern initiatives contributing to increasing the supply of water have, with time, included desalinating sea-water and treating waste water – and potentially reusing it for irrigation purposes, as has been done in Marrakesh recently (Imad Boulahat, 2020). Although technological advances have very much been associated with finding new means to increase the supply of water, managing water demand has been better linked to economic and social rationales, either through pricing and incentive systems, or through improved governance processes, as we will see in the next sections.

Modernity and economics

The modernization of the rural world

Before the Protectorate, most of the Moroccan territory was dominated by an extensive agropastoral system. As Jouve (2006) explained, during the "era of water from the sky", small-scale agricultural practices, inherited from Al-Andalus water management techniques, were very much dependant on climatic hazards, cautious and adapted to geographical variations. Whilst some land was used for agricultural purposes, vast areas, including forest-land, were shared by tribes on the basis of collective rights of pasture. Rural communities were therefore far from all being sedentary; many remained nomadic. As Lazarev (2014) explains, their very strong social structures resisted against the imposition of new agricultural authorities and practices. Traditionally, these structures were based on:

• An extremely weak "agrarian capitalism" – agricultural activities were aimed at feeding people and ensuring the survival of communities and entrepreneurial attitudes had no importance whatsoever.
• The predominance of the community, much more important than the individual, were – and still are – represented by the *Jmaa*, community of wise, elderly men responsible for the others.

It is this form of "institutional arrangement", whose rules and principles are based on solidarity and collectivity, that rural communities always referred to, as their main form of authority. In contrast, there has been a long tradition of mistrust from rural communities towards the *Makhzen*, perceived as the tax collector, potentially accompanied by destructive armies, or even prepared to steal land for the benefit of the colonizer (Marthelot, 1961).

Rural communities feared that, as the tractor was the weapon of the colonizer, modernization could well be the weapon of dispossession.

History shows that Moroccans are deeply rooted into their tribal, rural "bled". Although this factor considerably slowed down the modernization processes, the Protectorate nevertheless reached its objectives in various ways. First, legal reforms facilitated land status and ownership changes by promoting a speculative type of economy and land markets. Pasture-land (that belonged to nomadic tribes) were transformed into "collective land" which could be colonized. Second, a plethora of "modernization tools" were developed to try to attract rural communities to this new paradigm (Marthelot, 1961). A short- and medium-term compulsory credit system was put in place through the *Sociétés Indigènes de Prévoyance*, created in 1917, accompanied by a system of distribution of seeds and modern agricultural equipment. Attempts were made at generating a cooperative movement intended to promote a better integration of farmers into modern agricultural ways – but these movements disappeared in the 1950s. A third attempt at modernizing the traditional agropastoral community was to introduce new irrigation systems, through the management and authority of the Office de l'Irrigation des Beni Amri, (created in 1941) – to whom communities refused to obey.

Rather dissatisfied by these meagre results, the Protectorate moved up a gear by putting pressure on ecological environments – since humans were not accepting to change. By ensuring that rural communities were becoming sedentary elsewhere, the Protectorate institutions focused on transforming the land in order to make it more productive. The drainage of the "*merjdas*" marshland (representing 15,000 hectares in Kénitra and 5000 hectares in Ras Daoura) should have been accompanied by a set of measures aimed at helping nomadic tribes whose animals were originally dependent on these ecosystems. Instead, the communities were pushed on to less fertile land and, ultimately, had to leave the countryside to seek jobs in growing cities.

Engineering projects focused on "capturing" water from the mountains, in view of ensuring that the plains could be irrigated. This was done through the construction of a series of dams as well as the diversion of the enormous river called Oum Er Rbia via a 45-km long canal, a project that indigenous populations were strongly opposed to (Montligeon, 1932: 327). Whilst many dams built in the 1930s were used to generate hydroelectricity for growing cities and new industries, many were used to irrigate hectares of wheat – a grain that was much needed in France, which imported it at preferential rates. However, these fabricated tariffs did not reflect the fact that the land was not that fertile and that the productivity was pretty weak. In reality, these crops were costly. It is in this difficult context, and with the arrival of general Steeg who replaced Lyautey in 1925, that the "Californian dream" started. Steeg created the *Caisse de l'hydraulique Agricole* and sent professionals to California for them to learn how to grow and commercialize other new crops adapted to a semi-arid climate. From then on, new species (citrus fruits, vegetables, wine, cotton…) were selected for a more intensive type of agricultural production, by an also new *genre* of settlers belonging to a more private, entrepreneurial type of colonization. These new initiatives relied on the construction of larger dams.

In 1925, French settlers were already occupying 50% of the 1 million hectares they would ultimately occupy by the end of the Protectorate – the most fertile land. Moroccan farmers were focusing on local markets and paid the "*tartib*", tax which represented 20% of the State's revenue.

Since all action undertaken by the Protectorate was of a commercial nature, the Moroccan territory was progressively transformed into a network of roads and connections to ports, railtracks, and bridges, and coastal lands and plains were turned towards export activities. The rural world and the mountains became marginalized because "unproductive" and therefore considered as "useless", as opposed to the productive agricultural regions and the big cities (Casablanca, the "New York city" of Lyautey and Rabat, his "Washington city") that were part of the "useful Morocco" (his "Maroc Utile").

As El Jihad (2001) pointed out, it was as if the creation of economic wealth *depended on* the marginalization of "useless" areas. France had succeeded in *containing* the mountains that it had not succeeded in *conquering*, thanks to the support it had gained from the local *Caiids*. Whilst those benefited from the economic success of the colonizers, rural communities at large did not. Clearly, some communities were also more "useful" than others.

Water markets and public–private partnerships

Very rapidly in Morocco, the way in which water–human communities interactions was envisaged radically changed. Whilst, traditionally, water, as a gift from God, was effectively "managed" by the sky, it started being regulated and allocated by the State during the Protectorate and after the Independence and, in the 1980s, started entering the market sphere. In 30 years, a traditional, if not spiritual, understanding of this key natural resource, was completely turned upside down.

During the 1980s, a general trend towards the transformation, by the private sector, of public goods and services into market commodities started worldwide, initiated by numerous international institutions, such as the World Bank. One of the important factors behind such transformation was the rapid growth of cities, phenomenon from which a series of pressing preoccupations emerged – such as building infrastructures, creating functioning networks for water, sewage, electricity, waste management, etc. More often than not, public local and national financial capacities were insufficient to cope with these rapidly changing situations. In practice, this led to an institutional decentralization process, characterized by the creation of public–private partnerships and the identification of new roles for local authorities through contracts signed between them and private (often foreign) firms. Stakeholders involved in the management of water resources changed.

As early as during the Protectorate, cities like Casablanca and Rabat grew rapidly, receiving more and more people from the rural world, looking for work, homes, food, and sanitation. If the rural world was poor, the economic plans of the 1970s had not succeeded in reaching their objectives and, besides, were introducing new ideas (e.g., coastal mass tourism) suggested by foreign consulting firms, that seemed difficult to operationalize in the cultural context of North Africa at the time. The massive droughts of the 1980s did not help either, and social tension rose. The International Monetary Fund suggested new measures, promoting public–private partnerships and the delegation of urban services. The liberalization of the economy, privatization, and the disinvolvement of the State were core to the country's economic new strategies.

In water management, the private sector intervened in building small-scale dams (36 in the 1980s) and managing private irrigation systems based on the new reliance on groundwater. The massive shift from surface water to excessive groundwater usage contributed to ecological imbalances and difficulties in replenishing water reserves used for small farms. With water stress increasing dramatically in the 1990s, it became imperative to find ways of saving, recycling, and treating water. The technical know-how and financial management of these changes were put in the hand of the private sector through a system of *"gestion déléguée"* – half-public, half-private. This system had already been put in place in 1914 with the creation of the SMD (Moroccan Society for water, gas, and electricity distribution), managed by the *Lyonnaise des Eaux* (De Miras and Godard, 2006). In 1950, the SMD had ensured the creation and management of drinkable water distribution for Casablanca from the water derived from the Oum Er Rbia river.

Later, in the 1990s, when the management of services followed a completely liberal economic approach, concessions for the distribution of water in Tangier, Casablanca, Rabat, and Tétouan became the responsibility of four private companies. In 1997, the Lydec was put in charge of water, electricity, and sanitation in Casablanca. In 1998, Spanish and Portuguese companies had the same role to play in Rabat, replaced later by Véolia Water, in 2002. That same year, *Véolia Environnement Maroc* focused on Tangier and Tétouan, through a fusioned "régie" called Amendis (amen – or aman – meaning water, in Amazigh). The private sector intervened in the irrigation sector in 2002, boosted by the recommendations from the World Bank. This was done through the construction of a "transmission pipeline" (Guerdane project) and the construction of a water distribution network, in the Ghrab region.

All in all, as El Menouar (2012) points out, the privatization and delegation of the water and electricity services became a big business in a short period of time (1997–2002), both in terms of volumes of water being distributed (50% of the water was distributed by private companies in the cities) and in terms of revenue generated. Only accounting for

Rabat, Casablanca, Salé, Tangier, and Tétouan, the revenue generated by the distribution of water by private firms was estimated to be the equivalent of 2.5% of Morocco's GDP.

So, can the system of water *"gestion déléguée"* be considered as a success story in the modernization of water management in Morocco? Was following a market – supply and demand – logic helpful when dealing with growing urbanization, growing water needs … and growing water scarcity? The answer is rather negative.

Whilst social initiatives had to be undertaken to help the poorer communities connect to water, only 1250 connections (between 1997 and 2007), out of the 10,000 yearly connections that were planned, were effectively carried out and the cost of water and electricity connection remained way too high for the majority of city dwellers (Lahlou, 2010; El Menouar, 2012). For everybody to connect to the water network, social policies based on financial incentives should have been put into place. Companies were not interested in risky social groups: as a consequence, water services very rarely benefited to all.

If the social difficulties had been underestimated by the companies, so was the case concerning the extent of repair and infrastructure maintenance needed. For instance, despite a relatively high level of waste water collection (70% on average), only 5% of this water was being subjected to treatment – the rest was directly thrown into the ocean.

For De Miras and Godard (2006), the lessons that can be drawn from this modernization experience and, more specifically, that of the *"gestion déléguée"* are as follows: (1) private and public monopolies generate distortions in terms of prices and in the quality of the service. A broader conception of interactive regulation and governance is necessary and, for a win–win situation to emerge, local authorities, the State, and federated consumers all need to be involved. (2) More satisfactory and appropriate systems need to be found for the poorer communities to be taken into account in the delivery of such fundamental services. As these authors (2006) showed, *"public funding is always missing in what should, however, be public-private partnerships. Private actors cannot carry on being the only ones that are accountable in these commitments. Services companies are not bankers"* (p. 13).

Because of this, countries like Morocco, short of negotiating more realistic contracts and of taking part in initial investments, risk losing the potentially helpful contribution of foreign firms. Even recently (2016, 2017), demonstrations against water tariffs set by firms such as Lydec were making the headlines. The problem with matching market approach with services related to water is far from being solved.

Modernity and governance

As we saw in the previous two sections, modernizing the water management system was carried out through the use of new technology, based on a very different economic paradigm. This, in itself, had implications in terms of governance and so, the modernization of water governance took communities further away from the traditional social structures that had been put into place to manage conflicts, distribution, and maintenance.

Land management and advanced regionalization

The modernization of agriculture, rapid urbanization, and industrialization of the country separated both territory and communities into disconnected parts that did not correspond to neither geographical, climatic, nor ecological zones. In terms of environmental and water management, it mattered: for decades, the human–nature interactions went further away from each other rather than becoming more closely connected.

Whilst, before the Protectorate, water governance was guided by the customary laws of tribes, it was rapidly completely transformed to fit a differentiation system based on irrigation. Priority was given to the central plains and thirsty export crops. Meanwhile, mountain communities were more and more isolated, neglected and, ultimately, impoverished. As Roose et al. stressed (2010), the authorities never understood, nor explored, the traditional mountain agricultural systems and, instead, excluded them from what they saw as the "development of the rural world in Morocco". No investment was directed towards mountainous regions.

This was part of what Adidi described as a general set of imbalances observed at the end of the Protectorate that left Morocco *"with a disarticulated economy, a broken down territory, an un-finished urban system, a disproportionately big set of economic activities in the coastal area of Casablanca (75% of industries concentrated there) and a quarter of the urban population living in slums"* (2011: 4).

The first attempt to manage the Moroccan territory as a whole entity was done in the context of colonial urbanism, in the 1940s, when Michel Ecochard was asked to find ways to reduce urban congestion in the centre of Casablanca. After the independence, it became clear that decentralizing the economic activities would also depolarize the economic development of the country and, potentially, reduce inequalities and imbalances. But there was a very long way to go. Detaching the

country from one economic paradigm in view of installing a geographically more spread out set of activities and a less centralized governance
system was in fact harder to do than to recommend.

The evolution towards the less centralized *"Aménagement du
Territoire"* was arduous and took decades. The Report on "Advanced
Regionalization" (CCR 2011) retraced that evolution, from the
original definitions of *"Aménagement du territoire"* in the Plan
Quinquennal of 1968–1972, which was inclusive and participatory,
via the various splits of the country into 28 provinces and 7 regions,
in 1975, following the project of progressive regionalization (1971),
all the way to the more ambitious national debate on land management, in 1998. The National Strategy for Rural Development and
then the Report on Advanced Regionalization (with the creation of
16 regions), respectively, came out in 2007 and in 2010. On page 14,
the report stresses that, in terms of economic, social, cultural, and
environmental development, each domain (water, energy, and transport) is likely to be shared between the State and the various territorial *collectivities* (local authorities), in accordance to the principle
of subsidiarity (CCR, 2011).

From a land management perspective, the concept of sustainable
development was timidly being linked to territorial governance, in view
of enhancing social equity. The regional *collectivity* was the new key
stakeholder, favoured partner of the State, when it came to integrate
development plans at different levels.

Despite remarkable initiatives and the recognition of the fact that
regional imbalances had to be rectified, numerous criticisms of the
outcomes of the *Aménagement du territoire* have been expressed. As
Mateuh (1999) summarizes:

> the technical-state driven initiatives showed signs of weakness in
> two domains: society and the natural environment. Clearly, the
> existence of society was not ignored, but communities were treated
> in quantitative ways, using growth rates and percentages. People
> were considered as "objects" rather than "actors" in development
> processes. Nature was not ignored either but was considered as a
> "stock of resources" that needed to be used as much as possible, a
> set of forces that needed to be mastered.
>
> (1999: 8)

In terms of real changes in governance systems, authors such
as Adidi (2011), Mohaine (2017), Lazarev (2014), and many others,
emphasized that creating new institutions is not enough to ensure that

participation and decentralization can really take place in practice. To them, since the independence of the country, most policy-makers have had no idea concerning what a culture of sharing and listening would mean in the context of governance. Choosing people who will manage regions rather than having them elected is not democratic. Giving names to the new regions that do not reflect regional specificities but defines them in relation to the central power, does not give value to these regions and their inhabitants. As Lazarev (2014) demonstrated, during the Protectorate, and until now, the rural world has been perceived as needing to be controlled and mistrusted. Historically, "integrating the rural world" often meant creating alliances with traditional elites of the rural world who were keen to support the authority. In order to put in place a governance system based on people's participation "on the ground", the State will have to accept that, in geopolitical terms, any territory can become a geopolitical stakeholder who can make claims and express demands – something that the Moroccan State is reluctant to facilitate.

Regarding the protection of nature and the implementation of concepts such as sustainable development, new approaches focused on evaluation methods, such as environmental impact assessment methods. Putting them into practice, as Philipert (2015) showed, proved that it was not really helping to protect the environment, despite new laws (law 12-03) enforcing it, and generating systematic procedures. Only 40% of projects that should be submitted to an EIA process are effectively evaluated, most of the time after having started. Even worse, the projects that are considered as most critical for the economic development of the country, systematically escape the procedure. All in all, environmental quality comes second best after the economic competitivity of the region.

One can only hope that the ambitious objectives expressed in the 2011 Report will become real one day.

Decentralized governance and water management

As Houria Tazi Sadeq (2006) has shown, water is a core ingredient to land management in Morocco. She explains that *"the integration of the environmental, social and economic domains within AdT has been perceived as a considerable improvement, with water helping structure AdT"* (2006: 133).

The Ministry of Land management, Water and the Environment (MATEE) is set to be the main player in terms of water management strategies – although each ministry involved in water and sanitation matters also benefits from having administrative structures that represent them locally.

One of the objectives is to have a clear view on national water strategies (identified by the Inter-ministerial Commission on Water created in 2001). Another one is to coordinate the efforts of the various ministries involved in water issues. All in all, the State, effectively, is keeping a close eye on local affairs, despite the apparent wish to strengthen "decentralization".

Having said that, many initiatives have been carried out that are participatory in nature and have facilitated cooperation and the creation of partnerships on the ground in the domain of water management. Houria Tazi Sadeq, thus mentions the PAGER program, focused on the involvement of participants from the start of a project. Besides, numerous water user associations were created, following the 1990 Law n2-84 that emerged from the Dahir n1-87 (decree). In addition, water and environmental NGOs are multiplying and are much better connected to local communities, their needs, and their language than other official institutions: they know what will and what will not work.

However, introducing new institutional and social practices has not been easy, especially when participation has been "controlled". Examples of participatory projects that have been overlooked by individual interests unfortunately abound.

Maybe one sign of optimism lies in the creation of Basin Agencies that have nothing to do with an administrative "decoupage" of the country but, rather, follow a water, ecological basin logic that is not of a political nature. The identification of their role and functions, in relation to land management and to the centrality of water amongst interrelated environmental issues, has been central to reformed water laws and efforts to improve water governance in the future. The last chapter of Part III will illustrate potential avenues for this.

Conclusion

Pérennès (1993: 17) synthesized outcomes focused on colonial times in North Africa and showed that, in each case, although in different ways, the rapid modernization processes introduced resulted in very debatable, often negative, outcomes. In the specific context of Morocco, colonization disrupted the coherence of rural society, which became subject to new interests – those of the colons and of the French civil engineering companies. Water infrastructures were reorganized in view of meeting the colonial land management strategies. This led to series of conflicts between *seguia* users and Moroccan and French farmers, as documented by El Faiz and Ruf (2007) through the case study of the construction of the Nfis dam (1935). Marthelot (1961), who focused on the protectoral objective of modernization of the rural world through economic and technological improvements of agricultural systems, also drew quite pessimistic conclusions. Talking of the sedentarization of nomadic communities, in particular, he stressed that *"it has often been noticed that traditional societies, when exposed to a community that is technically more 'advanced', experienced a sclerosis of their customs and practices, accompanied by a growing poverty"* (Marthelot, 1961: 140).

As a whole, the modernization that the country experienced during the protectorate and that was further enhanced after the independence was perceived more like a shock than an improvement. The feeling of inefficiency, of disappointment, that comes out of writings on the "modernization of Northern Africa" highlights too many negative outcomes that did not match the initial expectations, or that did not meet neither Moroccan people nor colonial hopes or needs. Reflecting back on the post-independence project of modernization invites us to reflect on which other types of modernization could have possibly been opted for, for whose benefit and with which performance criteria.

Right now, at the beginning of the XXIst c., with water stress rapidly rising and serious geopolitical choices to be made, Morocco is in a position to question what development, economic success, and the sustainability and resilience of a country mean. Drawing lessons from previous experiences on "progress" could potentially help in reorientating the compass.

One lesson is that top-down approaches did not succeed in involving rural communities in the long-run. For modernism to be meaningful, it needs to have been shaped by the people who will live with this modernity and use the tools that have been designed to make it flourish. Another lesson is that a solid know-how already exists in the rural world, for which technologies are based on a socioecological logic and that is designed to be appropriate and resilient. Although there is a tendency to view traditional practices as being rigid and static, the Moroccan rural world is the first one to have to be reactive and constructive by learning how to adapt to changing climatic conditions and by innovating. The wealth of its know-how, of its ecological–economic heritage, has been neglected for long. Not integrating it into development strategies might have been one of the biggest mistakes.

Similarly, the modern "'nation-building programmes" have stigmatized any suggestion that Berber distinctiveness should have a place within North African independence movements. They have marginalized the countries' "Berberness" in favour of an Arab nationalist and Islamic identity, and chose to view Berber identity as a folkloric remnant useful for the tourist industry. And yet, it is probably through recognizing the wealth of know-how that both Berbers and Arabs have and can share in Morocco that the water of such a varied land will be best managed, in the most forward-looking type of developmental project.

References

Adidi, A. (2014) De l'aménagement du territoire au développement du territoire: quelle transition et quelle articulation? *1ère Conférence Intercontinentale d'Intelligence Territoriale "I.C.I. les territoires, l'Intelligence, la Communication et l'Ingénierie territoriales pour penser ensemble le développement des territoires"*, Gatineau 2011, Oct 2011, Gatineau, Canada. https://halshs.archives-ouvertes.fr/halshs-00960909, accessed on 16th of October 2020.

Bennis, A. and H. Tazi-Sadeq (1998) Population and irrigation water management: general data and case studies. In de Sherbinin, A., and Dompka and L. Bromley (Eds.) *Water and Population Dynamics. Case Studies and Policy Implications*. Washington, DC: AAAS. www.aaas.org/international/ehn/waterpop/morroc.htm accessed on 9th of October 2020

Commission Consultative de la Régionalisation (2011) *Rapport sur la régionalisation avancée*. Rabat: CCR.

De Miras, C. et X. Godard (2006) Les firmes concessionnaires de service public au Maroc: eau potable, assainissement et transports collectifs. *Méditerranée: Revue géographique des pays méditerranéens*. N. 106: 113–124.

Doukkali, M.R. (2005) Water institutional reforms in Morocco. *Water Policy*. 7 (1): 71–88.

Economie Entreprises (2020) *L'envasement entraine d'énormes pertes- entretien avec Imad Boulabat*. http://economie-entreprises.com/2020/05/07/lenvasement-entraine-denormes-pertes/ accessed on 15th of October 2020.

El Faiz, M. (2000) Le modèle de la Grande Hydraulique dans le Haouz de Marrakech. *Economies et Sociétés– Les usages de l'eau, échelles et modèles en Méditerranée*. N. 37.

El Faiz, M. and T. Ruf (2007) *La gestion collective de l'eau est-elle encore possible dans le Nfis à l'ouest de Marrakech?* https://hal.archives-ouvertes.fr/cirad-00154399 accessed on 16th of October 2020

El Ghomari, K. (2015) *Le bilan de la politique des barrages au Maroc*. www.barrages-cfbr.eu/IMG/pdf/07_-_el_ghomari_-politique_des_barrages_au_maroc.pdf accessed on 15th of October 2020

El Jihad, M. Moulay Driss (2001) L'eau de la montagne et le pouvoir étatique au Maroc; entre le passé et le présent. *Annales de géographie.* 110 (622): 665–672.

El Menouar, A. (2012) *Pour une gouvernance optimale de l'eau au Maroc.* Rabat: Imprimerie Bidadaoui.

Haut Commissariat au Plan HCP (2007) *Agriculture 2030 Quels avenirs pour le Maroc?* Rabat: HCP.

Ihazrir, A. (2009) La politique hydraulique marocaine à l'épreuve. Sécheresse et crise des identités rurales. In Ayeb, H., and Ruf, T., (Eds.) *Eau, pauvreté et crises sociales.* Marseille: IRD.

Jouve, A.M. (2006) Les trois temps de l'eau au Maroc. l'eau du ciel, l'eau d'Etat, l'eau privée. *Confluences Méditerranée.* 3 (58): 51–61.

Khrouz, D. (1992) La politique agricole du Maroc indépendant. In Santucci, J.C. (Ed.) *Le Maroc actuel. Une modernisation au miroir de la tradition? Institut de recherche et d'études sur les mondes arabes et musulmans.* Aix en Provence: Editions du CNRS.

Lahlou, M. (2010) La privatisation de l'eau au Maroc: premiers constats à partir de l'expérience de la Lyonnaise des Eaux à Casa. In *Partage des Eaux*: www. partagedeseaux.info/La-privatisation-de-l-eau-au-Maroc-premiers-constats-a-partir-de-l-experience accessed on 8th of October 2020

Lazarev, G. (2014) *Ruralité et changement social. Etudes sociologiques.* Rabat: Université Mohamed V Agdal, Edition et Impressions Bouregreg.

L'Opinion (2020) *Le défi de la lutte contre l'envasement.* Rabat: Mars. www. lopinion.ma/Le-defi-de-la-lutte-contre-l-envasement_a544.html accessed on 15th of October 2020.

Marthelot, P. (1961) Histoire et réalité de la modernisation du monde rural au Maroc. *Revue Tiers Monde.* 2 (6): 137–168.

Matheu, P. (1999) PDES Rapport définitif de la Commission thématique 'Aménagement du territoire et développement durable. In Pierre-Louis, L. et al. (Eds.) *Le développement durable: un concept planétaire au risque de dynamiques territoriales.* Paris: Ministère de l'équipement – PUCA et Ministère de l'écologie et du développement durable.

Mikhail, A. (2013) *Water on Sand. Environmental Histories of the Middle East and North Africa.* Oxford: Oxford University Press.

Ministère de l'Énergie, des Mines, de l'Eau et de l'Environnement, Département de l'Environnement (MEMEE-DE, 2011) *Indicateurs du Développement durable du Maroc: Rapport National 2011.* Rabat: MEMEE-DE.

Mohaine, A. (2017) *La géographie et l'aménagement au Maroc.* Casablanca: Regards Croisés; Afrique Orient.

Montligeon sous la direction de Albert de Pouvourville (1932) *Histoire populaire des colonies françaises – le Maroc.* Paris: Editions du Velin d'or.

Pérennès, J. (1993) *L'eau et les hommes au Maghreb. Contribution à une politique de l'eau en Méditerranée.* Paris: Karthala.

Philifert, P. (2015) Aménagement et développement durable au Maroc: une longue marche ou une nouvelle donne? In Dupret, B. et al. (Eds.) *Le Maroc au présent.* Rabat: Centre Jacques Berque. pp 103–113.

Roose, E., M. Sabir and A. Laouina (2010) *Gestion durable de l'eau et des sols au Maroc. Valorisation des techniques traditionnelles méditerranéennes.* Marseille: IRD.

Tazi Sadeq, H. (2006) *Du droit de l'eau au droit à l'eau au Maroc et ailleurs.* Casablanca: La Croisée des Chemins.

Part III

New paths in water management

Towards alternative development

Introduction

The year is 2020. The world has entered a massive pandemic that has pushed us to question our reliance on globalization, technological fixes, short-termism, and our ignorance regarding ecological systems. Both human immunity systems and the resilience of economic systems have become main preoccupations. If "things will never be as they used to be", we need to identify how we could manage our societies and their interaction with the natural environment better, from now on. This opportunity to rethink development objectives, means, and actors is entirely relevant in the context of research on how to manage scarce natural resources such as water, in decades to come.

In a country like Morocco, which is entirely independent for water resources, is extremely rich in renewable resources, has a relatively stable political regime, a parliamentary monarchy, which asserts a strong will to democratize the running of the country by, for instance, putting into place an advanced type of regionalization, embracing a new type of development based on forward-looking principles aligned with XXIst c. constraints and context seems feasible and desirable. Traditionally inclined to follow France's steps, Morocco has now the potential to rediscover itself in the context of a new challenging geo-political setting. Keen to be an exemplary leader for other African countries, it is also progressively opening itself to the Anglo-Saxon world. However, harsh constraints are going to push the government to rethink the way it is running the country's affairs. In this third part, the following question is being asked: which socioecological economic alternatives could the semi-arid country of Morocco opt for in order to save its main source of life: water? The current constraints that it is facing suggest that finding alternative ways to develop the countries and more efficient, ecologically adapted, and socially orientated practices is not an option but rather an obligation. This obligation is not only ecologically driven but also politically and socially orientated: following the Arab Spring experienced in neighbouring countries, and a tepid attempt at an "advanced regionalization system", concerns and discontent are being more and more expressed by the people. If the needs of Moroccan people (in terms of food security, job, moves towards a more democratic type of governance and institutions) are to be met and a relative economic balance is to be found, alternative ways to define "modernity" need to be found.

Chapter 5 focuses on how the various problems generated by climate change are encouraging people to rethink "development strategies" and the meaning of "sustainable development", especially in the context of water management. Talking about water in a semi-arid country such as Morocco inevitably leads one to observe the ways in which it contributes to development and to look for the type of development path that seems most appropriate socially, politically, economically, and environmentally. In practice, climate change, for a country like Morocco, means increased desertification, water scarcity, but also the realization that the country is rich in renewable energies, the usage of which could benefit other countries and bring foreign currencies, as well as benefit Morocco itself by diminishing its fossil fuel dependency. Actions related to climate change do not particularly have to lead to diminishing the country's carbon and greenhouse gases emissions: from that perspective, the country is actually pretty "clean". To a large extent, acting against climate impacts must, rather, lead to changes in water management practices. By doing so, Morocco could provide exemplary pilot studies in water management practices for other African countries and hence, as an environmental leader, could boost a shift in the country's geopolitical positioning.

Acting on CC in Morocco therefore has a lot to do with improving water management practices. This is true because, whilst the Moroccan people struggles to apprehend what CC and sustainable development mean from the prestigious international conferences focused on these issues and often held in their own country, they, however, perfectly understand problems related to water, because they relate to them. It is thanks to changes in water that the country might therefore introduce the notion of sustainable development goals, to which the government is, at least in theory, so attached. It is also through critical issues related to water that various stakeholders will demonstrate that improvements do not come without a better governance, more equal economic objectives, and more participatory practices.

Chapter 6 in Part III highlights the fact that some traditional indigenous approaches are particularly well adapted and that we could learn from their resilient characteristics. One important emphasis is the "appropriateness" of technologies, both with regards to them respecting the ecological milieu but also in relation to the stakeholders who use them and are supposed to benefit from them. Many technological options selected to promote modern water management in Morocco, during and after the Protectorate, were based on heavy infrastructure and investments. Imposed from the top, they not only divided communities (some had access to them; some not) but also disempowered rural populations who did not understand the logic of these new approaches and refused to embrace them. So, what makes one "water technology" more appropriate than another?

Appropriate technology has been defined by Hazeltine and Bull (2003) as any object, process, idea, or practice that enhances human fulfilment through the satisfaction of human needs. It is appropriate when it is compatible with local, cultural, and economic conditions and utilizes locally available materials and energy resources, with tools and processes maintained and operationally controlled by the local population. To be "appropriate", a technology should also therefore be self-sustaining, cause little cultural disruption, and should ensure the relevance of technology to the welfare of the local population. Part III of the book investigates how traditional water management techniques could be revived so that they could meet current needs in the context of current constraints.

The adoption of technologies in a society goes hand in hand with a system of governance that accompanies decision-making processes and strategic choices. Changes in technologies and strategies therefore relate to changes in governance systems, a theme also covered in Part III. Governance is key to tackling water challenges and transforming water management under the increasing pressures of competing water uses, climate change, as well as new constraints imposed by the World Covid-19 pandemic that we are currently experiencing. If climate change has led to upset ecological patterns, with increased desertification in places and enhanced risks of flooding in others, if competition for water resources has become even fiercer in arid and semi-arid areas, the pandemic is also raising a plethora of uneasy questioning about our current food systems, weak immunity, and reliance on globalization. "Environmental governance" has attempted to introduce environmental considerations and actors into the sphere of decision-making and strategy-setting in various ways around the world. Authors such as Ozerol et al. (2018) undertook the huge task of synthesizing existing water governance systems and to explore their performance, insights, and potentials. Drawing lessons from various places, they concluded that four areas need particular attention if water governance is to be improved. The first one deals with improving the balance between small-, medium-, and large-scale governance. The second relates to temporal governance trends and patterns. Then the authors suggest that comparative studies, including those within the global south, could help design better water systems. Finally, *"addressing the issues of justice, equity, and power, are becoming increasingly important in tackling the water governance challenges that are exacerbated by the effects of climate change, industrialization, and urbanization"* (2018: 1). Out of the numerous publications they reviewed, Ozerol et al. noticed that "water governance" is seldom being given an overall definition (it can focus, on the other hand, on specific dimensions of water governance instead) (2018: 4). One of the rare definitions they found was formulated by Pahl-Wostl et al. (2012: 25, quoted in Ozerol et al. 2018: 4) who defined water governance as *"a system with structural features and transient processes at both rule making and operational levels,"* that *"takes into account the different actors and networks that help formulate and implement water policy."* One recurrent issue related to improved water governance relates to the participation of stakeholders and therefore to water justice. Boelens, Vos, and Perreault (2018: 2), who worked on this issue, stressed that:

> the combination of intensified resource extraction, land and water degradation, increasing competition over water access and control, and growing reliance on market forces and forms of water expertocracy, have profound implications for debates over water rights and justice. It is increasingly clear that water scarcity and insecurity are not so much related to the absolute availability of fresh and clean water, but rather are expressions of how water, and water services, are unequally distributed among societal groups.

There is an urgent need to question the modernization and development paths followed for a century and to suggest ways of integrating socioecologically appropriate technologies into more just systems of water governance. Part III explores how indigenous approaches to water management could help adapt to new constraints in order to provide more appropriate technology and governance systems that better involve stakeholders at appropriate scales.

References

Boelens, R., J. Vos, and T. Perreault (2018) Introduction: the multiple challenges and layers of water justice struggles. In Boelens, R., Perreault, T., and Vos, J. (Eds.) *Water Justice.* pp. 1–32. Cambridge: Cambridge University Press.

Hazeltine, B. and C. Bull (2003) *Field Guide to Appropriate Technology.* Cambridge MA: Academic Press.

Ozerol, G. et al. (2018) Comparative studies of water governance: a systematic review. *Ecology and Society.* 23 (4): 43.

5 Climate change, water stress, and the need for a new development paradigm

Climate change and the water crisis

The effects of climate change in Morocco

The semi-arid nature of Morocco is being negatively enhanced by Climate Change. In 2014, the Minister delegate of the Ministry of Energy, Mines, Water and Environment indicated that the climate projections foresaw an increase in average summer temperatures of 2–6°C and a 20% decline in average rainfall by the end of the century. These vulnerabilities will go increasing with the growing needs of the population and industries.

Olborode Jegede explained that, in Africa:

> climate change contributes to a lack of viability of indigenous peoples' lands, leads to migration, and thus makes their lands vacant for state occupation for use to serve national economic ends. (...) The Berbers of North Africa face an extreme scarcity of water, the degradation of palm trees, a deterioration of a unique tree species in south-western Morocco and salinisation in a changing climate.
>
> (2016: 202, 203)

Like many countries "from the South", Morocco seems to suffer more from the effects of climate change than to contribute to it. In 2004, the energy sector was responsible for over 52% of the global emissions of greenhouse gases in the country, followed by agriculture, with 31%. In total, Morocco produced 75 Mt CO_2 in 2004, making it one of the lowest emitting countries in the MENA (MEMEE, 2014: 14, 16). For many stakeholders "on the ground", such as rural communities, an event like the COP 22 held in Marrakesh in 2016 was 'from another world', and the notions of climate change or of sustainable development way too conceptual. Instead, what are very real to them are the practical consequences of climate change. For instance, decreases of 3–30% rainfall were observed in the last decade. This trend is of course worrying for a country whose agriculture is not only important economically and culturally, but also because this sector is currently using 88% of the water resources available in the country (against a 70% world average). Better agricultural practices desperately need to be designed in view of tackling climate change and of designing development strategies that are better adapted to changes (natural, economic, political). Adopting a "business as usual" attitude would simply be detrimental to the country, where the agricultural sector is of high importance for the economy and particularly for poor people. Schilling et al. (2012) have shown that agricultural incentives used in the past have been inadequate to buffer drought effects and that new strategies should focus on developing resilience against climate change as well as agricultural policies that shift from maximizing agricultural output to stabilizing it.

Approaches undertaken to fight climate change

Major efforts to fight climate change have been undertaken in Morocco through a variety of texts, legal measures, and investments. The vision for a Moroccan Climate change policy has been elaborated to ensure a transition towards low carbon development activities. It is coherent with the National Strategy for Sustainable Development (2014) and is aimed at guiding public actions and initiatives. In terms of water and agricultural management, this led to responses that can be related to climate change *adaptation* or *mitigation*. As Oluborode Jegede explains, "*Adaptation is the adjustment or response that moderates harm or exploits beneficial opportunities in climate change, whereas mitigation connotes human intervention to reduce the sources or enhance the sinks of greenhouse gases*" (2016: 105).

In Morocco, measures taken followed adaptation strategies. Climate change can become more meaningful to stakeholders on the ground when explored through the *effects* that CC generates (e.g., water scarcity) or the *ways in which CC can be slowed down* (e.g., through generating less pollution, and less waste). Strategies to do so might help a whole range of stakeholders feel better equipped and more capable of tackling the huge overall problem of CC.

In theory, Morocco is committed to proactively implement adaptation and mitigation actions as part of an integrated participatory and responsible approach (MEMEE, 2014). The Moroccan National Water Strategy completed in 2009 identified, in line with the main Policy on

Climate Change in Morocco (2014) nine strategic areas for CC adaptation (water resources, agriculture, fisheries, forestry, health, biodiversity, tourism, urbanism, and land development).

Previously, the 2007 Morocco Green Plan for agriculture had worked on developing adaptive capacities of rural populations. The National Irrigation water saving program was thus planned to introduce drip irrigation over an area of 555,000 ha (which would save 1.4 billion m^3/year) by 2020 (MEMEE, 2014: 30). Overall, from 2005 to 2010, 64% of CC related spending was related to climate adaptation (PSACC and GIZ, 2018).

Oluborode Jegede cautioned that *"global CC response initiatives have a potentially negative impacts on indigenous peoples' land tenure and use"* and that *"none of the National Adaptation Plans prepared by African States indicated the special situation of indigenous people's lands in the context of CC"* (2016: 105). In Morocco, the connection between CC adaptation strategies and indigenous knowledge on resilient agricultural practices was certainly not made, until a number of people dared questioning the outcomes of modern water and agricultural management and to suggest that alternative development practices might help the country to identify more sustainable ways to meet its needs.

The need for alternative development and water management approaches

What modern water management brought to Morocco

The modernization of water and agricultural management manifested itself through land management, choice of cultures, and irrigation. As discussed in Chapter 4, strategies based on major investments and infrastructure dominated; the Moroccan society came out of this "experiment" broken and disorientated.

In terms of land management, "modern times" came with the rise of a powerful Moroccan administration that replaced that of the Protectorate and transferred colonial land to State administrations or civil or military personalities. Only 30% of previous colonial lands ended up in the hands of small-scale landowners developing subsistence agriculture. Agricultural equipment benefited the bigger landowners and so did the tax relief systems put into place, increasing even further the already big inequalities in the rural world (Lazarev, 2014: 14).

In view of modernizing agricultural practices, the State decided to introduce new crops by inventing a system of contract that would set a fixed price for agricultural products as well as a compensation scheme in case of droughts. This system was based on growing cotton, beet-root, and tomatoes, at an industrial scale. With regards to irrigation, the State-funded new irrigation equipment, and specified that farmers were legally obliged to progressively reimburse part of the sums invested in this equipment and – unwelcome novelty – to pay for the water they consumed. The attempt to combine traditional to modern irrigation techniques failed and the targets that had been set by the agricultural strategy could not be reached. To remedy this, King Hassan II decided to considerably increase the irrigation ambitions of the country by promising, thanks to the construction of numerous dams, that 1 million hectares could be irrigated by 2020.

In view of ensuring the integration of these three elements (land, crops, water) and their management by a bigger and more diverse community of farmers, the National Promotion (PN) encouraged the contribution of "small stakeholders" to meeting the bigger national requirements and objectives of intensification, industrialization, and exports. A large proportion of workers would contribute to these enterprises – such as well digging, reforestation, construction of water retention structures – rather than machinery. This would create jobs and generate incomes for families that land reforms had displaced. However, as Khrouz explained, "*the PN was unfortunately an unsuccessful oper-ation which introduced a civil-servant mentality in farmers' communities who, disempowered, saw their ancestral know-how being de-valued*" (1992: 120). For agricultural communities, who were used to basing their strategies on subsistence agriculture, and for whom polycultures were the best response to a precarious, harsh, and high-risk natural envir-onment, export cash crops, agricultural credits, and rural exodus had emerged from Sate's choices that were both foreign and incomprehen-sible to them. They did not belong to a "field-work", practical type of reasoning. Nothing, in modern Moroccan society, had prepared rural communities to integrate these approaches into their paradigm.

Analysing the specific shortcomings derived from the majority (75%) of great development projects focused on water and soil con-servation allowed Roose and his IRD team (2010) to understand the causes for their repeated failure. First, the farmers, main managers of the land, were not involved on the development of the projects that the technicians who adopted a top-down approach. Second, the techniques adopted did not take account of the specificities and variety of types of erosion and socioecological systems already in place.

Since the mid-1980s, Roose et al. (2010) have developed methods that target better rural communities' needs. They concluded that it is not relevant nor realistic to aim at developing one universal method.

Rather, by examining which practices have been traditionally developed over centuries and adapting them to new agronomic and soil conservation methods, the improvement of soil quality can actually allow to double agricultural production every 20 years, whilst improving the rural environment by taking better care of fragile lands (Roose et al. 2010: 17).

Towards alternative development – implications for water strategies

The evolution of modernization and development theories

Commenting on what happened to decolonized African and British countries after their independence, Cooper explained that not only modernization proceeded along several "key axes"[1] but also that these axes jointly evolved. Industrialism was not limited to industry; it had become a way of life, and modernity constituted a package. The study of post-war, post-colonization "modern" processes became closely linked to that of "development".

As Lewis explained:

> Development in its modern sense first came to official prominence when it was used by United States President Truman in 1949 as part of the rationale for post-War reconstruction in "underdeveloped" areas of the world, based on provision of international financial assistance and modern technology transfer. Development has subsequently been strongly associated primarily with economic growth.
>
> (Lewis, 2005: 474)

This controversial concept is considered as *"an organised system of power and practice which has formed part of the colonial and neo-colonial domination of poorer countries by the West"* (Lewis, 2005: 474).

The post-war link between development and growth largely remains valid, especially in the priority structural adjustments advocated by international agencies such as the International Monetary Fund, the World Bank, and the World Trade Organisation – which locates development within the reform of international trade regulations and the freer movement of capital between North and South. Besides, the technological paradigm of development remains stronger than ever in the biotechnology movement, which still promises technological fixes to development problems in agriculture.

In reaction to this, new schools of thoughts have developed. Thus, as Lewis explained (2005), the "dependency theories" rejected the modernization paradigm and focused instead on the unequal relation-ship between North and South. It argued that an active process of "underdevelopment" had taken place, as peripheral economies were integrated into the capitalist system on unequal terms, primarily as providers of cheap raw materials for export to rich industrialized coun-tries. The 1990s also led to the integration of anthropology into devel-opment debates. Applied anthropologists have greatly contributed to development work by drawing attention to issues of Western bias in the assumptions that inform development initiatives, uncovering areas of cultural difference, and highlighting the value of local, practical, or "indigenous" knowledge. To them, development interventions should be informed by the systems of knowledge recognized by local indi-genous people.

The debate on how to best approach "development" issues evolved throughout time and led to the creation of new paradigms that explored the concept not only in the context of the "developing world". Thus, *"recently, courageous influential and practical attempts to bring together the analysis of ecology, economy and social behaviour in rich economies have begun to emerge. Particularly noteworthy is Tim Jackson's book Prosperity without growth: economies for a finite planet 2011"* (Healy et al., 2013: 529). These contributions represent the emergence of a new ecological macroeconomics, linked to political ecology and mul-tiple languages of valuation. Community-based management is a related concept that refers to forms of cooperation in management of natural resources where dialogue, discussion, and deliberation among the interested parties are key elements (Carlsson and Berkes, 2005). Similarly, resilience-based approaches that acknowledge the difficulty to forecast the future in a meaningful way and the need to maintain the capacity of a system to absorb a shock or to reorganize after a major perturbation are contributing more and more to "development initiatives".

Alternative development and sustainable water management

To what extent can these new schools of thoughts help us to define what sustainable development means in the context of water management? That water is necessary in all forms of development is well known and not controversial: water is needed in all forms of activity, and has no substitute. In addition, as was explained by Icomos:

the major development options of human societies determine the structure of their relationship to water, but at the same time, hydrological, geographic and geological data determine the major sociotechnical choices which make them possible, or sometimes impossible, and make them sustainable or unsustainable.

(2017: 16)

This two way set of factors is a dynamic relationship, both affected by natural constraints and sociopolitical choices.

When trying to define sustainable water management, people agree that integrated, participatory management systems, that take account of both ecological habitats and human communities, can help manage a scare resource and potential conflicts rising from competitive uses. This description attempts to be universal but does not help in specific settings.

In a context of global trade in agricultural commodities, that has boosted fresh water consumption and the export of "virtual water", Vos and Boelens (2014) explain that *"recent initiatives to certify agricultural production are showing a rapidly growing interest in considering water issues within schemes of quality assurance, sustainable production and fair trade"* (Vos and Boelens, 2014: 206). This is because local communities and ecosystems, especially in arid regions, have been very negatively affected by this global trade. However, the authors observed that certain sustainability standards have generated problems – showing validity for some stakeholders more than for others.

Vos and Boelens (2014) critically examined several certification schemes to incorporate control points related to water use and/or water pollution (e.g., GlobalGAP, MPS-ABC, the Rainforest Alliance, and IFOAM). They concluded that the international private certification schemes have significant flaws when it comes to operationalizing sustainable and/or fair production and trade of agricultural products. In particular:

> they fail to deal adequately with the spatial and social diversities that underlie local livelihood strategies, agro-environmental production processes and water control problems and introduce standards that either exclude, or align, normalize and 'correct' production practices according to the interests of transnational agrofood chains.

(2014: 225)

If modes of certification carry on existing and are to impact on the sustainability of modes of production, they should be based on schemes that recognize local or regional diversity and elaborate on context-based conceptualizations of sustainability and ecological justice. In order for these schemes to not be left to the initiative of external food companies, water user communities who are most at stake need to take part in sharing their understanding of what sustainable water practices entail. This new involvement should be part of changes in water governance systems. As Icomos (2017) stressed, hydraulic systems evolve over time and changes and adaptations to them need to take place for resilience to occur.

> Hydraulic systems are constantly readjusted to suit user demand, depending on the accessible resources. This ability to adapt is a condition for their sustainability (...). Evolutions and technical changes form an integral part of their history, which is not only the history of their design and their period of origin (...). These adaptations (...) have occurred both for heritages which are still living and for those which are today archaeological remains or relict landscapes.
>
> (Icomos, 2017: 19)

Like Adeel et al. (2008), Icomos strongly recommends that, for sustainable water management to be more realistically defined and contextually appropriate, indigenous traditional knowledge on water management is carefully reexamined and that lessons are being drawn from it. As they explain:

> traditional knowledge has two salient features; it leads to practices that are: (a) socially acceptable; and (b) linked to sustainable utilization and management of natural resources. The latter point is particularly crucial for drylands where sustainability of water resources – in the face of inherent scarcity, wide-ranging fluctuation on a seasonal and annual basis and potential conflicts and competition amongst users – is a matter of life and death.
>
> (Adeel et al. 2008: 5)

Water as heritage and alternative water management

The next chapter will present how a set of traditional water management methods could be adapted to current constraints and help to draw useful lessons in the design of new water management practices. This section, however, suggests an alternative way of looking at water all together, that is: taking *water heritage* as a catalyst for new sources of revenue, other than those based on the production of crop exports.

In Morocco, the current pandemic, aside from its obvious health consequences on the population, is having disastrous effects on various economic sectors – tourism is one of them. In parallel, a long-lasting series of environmental crises related to climate change had already jeopardized agricultural activities. In both sectors, new approaches towards water management could help find alternatives to old development models that do not seem to help in the current context. An alternative approach to tourism, more orientated towards cultural heritage, could help to develop the industry and revive some know-how that is being lost.

As Faouzi (2019) explains:

> the articulation between heritage and tourism could be a vector of territorial development, especially in places such as the Souss where tourism is under-developed, despite an important water patrimonial potential – mixing peasants' irrigation techniques and the history of great dynasties (Almoravids, Almohads, Saadies).
>
> (p. 491)

Of course, each region in Morocco has its own water heritage and discovering them would highlight a great cultural diversity. The current changes observed in the global economy is potentially facilitating the commercialization of elements that, so far, were not valued. Cultural tourism is one form of development that could ensure the joint and coherent durability of tourism and cultural heritage. Despite UNESCO's continuous efforts, it is only after the 2002 Johannesburg Summit that culture started being recognized as a real pillar of development. In Morocco, certain public services were created to deal with this, but further efforts and research are needed to ensure that a better governance of culture and natural resources is ensured. As Faouzi recommends, *"any strategy to link cultural heritage to economic activities must be based on the consolidation of decentralisation, citizens' participation, and the creation of institutions that will be capable of protecting and valuing cultural heritage"* (2019: 510).

Access to water is the premise to all forms of life, for all human civilizations.

> A return to traditional cultural heritages linked to water could help to provide assistance for recognising, studying and preserving heritage of this type (...) as well as providing a methodology for the identification and then the preservation of such heritage. This could be done in a wider context to establish benchmark examples, for the

benefit of everyone, and whose transmission to future generations could be assured in an appropriate way.

(Icomos, 2017: 10)

Such research could lead to the creation of *"a thesaurus of sustainable solutions whose tangible, social and energy costs are reasonable when compared to the extreme responses of contemporary techno-science applied to the field of water"* (Icomos, 2017: 11). Whilst Icomos worked at describing in detail the evolution of hydraulic systems throughout centuries and continents, valuing indigenous practices, in Morocco, a remarkable initiative was successfully undertaken through the creation of the Aman Water museum in Marrakesh, which beautifully presents what water management practices were developed, how and by whom, from pre-Islamic times until now.

This integration of natural resource management into the cultural sphere is totally new for our times – although, as El Faiz (2015) emphasized, water and agricultural practices were entirely integrated into spiritual, legal, and even artistic activities during the Al-Andalous era (Xth c.–XIVth c.). Revisiting the agronomic principles of that era, El Faiz never stopped stressing that the Al-Andalous understanding of economic activities had nothing to do with modern economics and commercial activities. Characterized by an interconnection of activities and actors, such "oikonomia"-based system was primarily aimed at meeting the needs of all in the community – an objective that seems lost in economic systems whose survival is based on inequalities.

Conclusion

The climactic and socioeconomic constraints that the rural world is facing today are such that finding new ways to manage scarce water resources has become an imperative. More than just "one-off" solutions, it is a change in paradigm that must be found to allow society to go beyond an era of modernization based on market dynamics and societal imbalances.

In Africa, Cooper (2004), who examined post-colonial development, suggests that:

the question that comes to mind is no longer what kind of social science an era of decolonization demands, but what kind of social science is needed for an era that people in Africa are experiencing as one of marginalization and despair?

(Cooper, 2004: 31)

This marginalization and impoverishment, indigenous rural communities of Morocco know it too well, and the efforts progressively and sporadically undertaken by the government to face these issues could well come from an anxiety that people might, in the end, protest against their situation in potentially violent uprises.

Traditional agriculture carries on being practiced by a large part of the rural population who depends on it for its livelihood. It never benefited from any substantial financial help. Nevertheless it survived. Can we carry on concentrating the main financial investments in great irrigation projects aimed at promoting the interests of a hegemonic agroexport sector? Reforming agricultural and water management practices in Morocco will necessarily imply questioning the type of management that has devalued water and agricultural heritage and neglected its innovative and resilient potential.

It is by building on the agro-technical arabo-andalus heritage in view of meeting the basic needs of large communities that Morocco will be able to rightly claim to belong of the scientific Nabatean agronomy tradition of Ibn Bassal and Ibn Awwam.

(El Faiz, 2015: 239)

Note

1 To him, modernization was a change from: a subsistence economy to an industrial exchange economy; rural to urban societies; a political system of subjects to one of citizens; notions of status to notions of achievement; extended to individualized units; religious ideologies to secular ideologies; diffuse, personalized relationships to contractual ones (Cooper, 2004: 26).

References

Adeel, Z., B. Schuster and H. Bigas (2008) *What Makes Traditional Technologies Tick?* Ontario: United Nations University, INWEH.

Carlsson, L. and F. Berkes (2005) Co-management: concepts and methodological implications. *Journal of Environmental Management.* 75 (1): 65–76.

Cooper, F. (2004) Development, modernization, and the social sciences in the era of decolonization: the examples of British and French Africa. *Revue d'histoire des Sciences Humaines.* 1(10): 9–38. www.cairn.info/revue-histoire-des-sciences-humaines-2004-1-page-9.htm, accessed on 29th September 2020.

El Faiz, M. (2015) *Agronomie et agronomes d'Al Andalous (XI–XIVe s.).* Casablanca: La croisée des chemins.

Faouzi, H. (2019) Hydraulic heritage of the upstream Souss, Morocco: untapped territorial resource. *Journal of Tourism and Heritage Research.* 2 (3): 491–451.

Healy, H. et al. (Eds) (2013) *Ecological Economics from the Ground Up.* London: Earthscan. p. 1–32 and p. 513–538.

ICOMOS (2nd edition) (2017) *Cultural Heritages of Water in the Middle East and Maghreb.* Charenton-Le-Pont: UNESCO, ICOMOS.

Khrouz, D. (1992) La politique agricole du Maroc indépendant. In Santucci, J.C. (Ed.) *Le Maroc actuel. Une modernisation au miroir de la tradition? Institut de recherche et d'études sur les mondes arabes et musulmans.* Aix en Provence: Editions du CNRS.

Lazarev, G. (2014) *Ruralité et changement social. Etudes sociologiques.* Rabat: Université Mohamed V Agdal, Edition et Impressions Bouregreg.

Lewis, D. (2005) Anthropology and development: the uneasy relationship. In Carrier, J.G. (Ed.) *A Handbook of Economic Anthropology.* Cheltenham: Edward Elgar. pp. 472–486.

Ministère délégué auprès du Ministre de l'Energie, des Mines, de l'Eau et de l'Environnement (2014) *L'engagement du Maroc dans la lutte contre les effets du changement climatique.* Rabat: CléConcept.

Oluborode Jegede, A. (2016) *The Climate Change Regulatory Framework and Indigenous Peoples' Lands in Africa: Human Rights Implications.* Pretoria: Pretoria University Law Press.

PSACC (Global program on private sector adaptation to Climate change) and GIZ (2018) *Climate Expert – Morocco.* www.climate-expert.org/en/home/ business-adaptation/morocco/, accessed on 15th of October 2020.

Roose, E., M. Sabir and A. Laouina (2010) *Gestion durable de l'eau et des sols au Maroc. Valorisation des techniques traditionnelles méditerranéennes.* Marseille: IRD.

Schilling J., K. P. Freier, E. Hertig and J. Scheffran (2012) Climate change, vulnerability and adaptation in North Africa with focus on Morocco. *Agriculture, Ecosystems and Environment.* 156: 12–26.

Vos, J. and R. Boelens (2014) Sustainability standards and the water question. *Development and Change.* 45 (2): 205–230.

6   Appropriate technologies

Managing water scarcities in the XXIst c.

Old technologies, new constraints

Rehabilitating the old khetarras

During the 1970s, the "First Hydraulic generation" in Morocco relied on three simple water management systems that were ecologically well-adapted, but also labour intensive, and reliant on heavy mainten-ance and know-how. In the Haouz plain, in particular, in the region of Marrakesh, they were organized as follows.

- The *seguias*, using surface water from the rivers flowing down from the Atlas mountains, watered 63% of irrigated fields.
- The *khettaras* watered 14% of irrigated surfaces and extracted more than 60% of groundwater, helping the drainage of swamps in the eastern part of Marrakesh and functioning as a self-regulating system, by reducing the level of water extraction during the low water period, and increasing it when the level of the water table was higher.
- The wells contributed to 3% of the irrigation.
- Mixed combined systems dealt with 15% of the surface.

These systems, based on the ecological recharge of the aquifers, also involved communities for their construction and maintenance, reinfor-cing solidarity within the community. This is why water collect through the *khetarra* system has been considered as a sustainable water manage-ment method. Historically, the "sustainable" dimension indeed passed the test of time since, as El Faiz documented:

> the network of khetarras has been developed since the era of Al Andalous and spread through North Africa, covering many

thousands of kilometres and ensuring the survival of an important rural community. One therefore understands the relevance of revisiting the works of Al Karajî who described all the details related to the construction of these underground galleries, as well as the numerous benefits they bring.

(El Faiz, 2015: 231)

The "Second hydraulic generation" ("la Grande Hydraulique") put into place in the 1980s generated a brutal sociopolitical shock between rural populations and the administrations in charge of the investments and loans delivered by the World Bank (El Faiz, 2001). In addition to these, ecological risks of a complete drainage of groundwater resources through overusages of water pumps were identified by Lightfoot (1996) who, together with other authors, advocated a study of possible reuse of the *khetarras*. To that aim, a group of researchers carried out the Isiimm (Institutional and Social Innovations in Irrigation Mediterranean Management) project between 2003 and 2007 and the Desmeth initiative (Development of the Mediterranean Societies, and of water territories), between 2005 and 2007.

These studies facilitated the reporting of thousands of years of orally transmitted know-how on ecologically sound water management and allowed to share this knowledge which, so far, had not been communicated outside rural communities. In the 1990s, the nature of the links between water management and the reforms of rural structures started being questioned again, after having been excluded from critical debates on the marginalisation of the rural world. This new questioning arose from the fact that the World Bank requested the creation of Water users Associations prior to delivering new loans (El Alaoui, 2004). The participation of more varied stakeholders thanks to these associations, as well as better documented ecological reports, helped to explain the shortcomings of the Grande Hydraulique.

El Faiz and Ruf (2007) showed that water management based on large-scale infrastructure and technology completely underestimated the needs for water whilst overestimating the ecological availability of water, leading to a never-ending water deficit. In addition, badly calculated risks of siltation, technical choices that were energy-costly as well as crops that were ill-adapted to the climate in the Haouz region, resulted in contradictions and injustices. The land speculation processes allowed foreigners to buy pieces of land that were traditionally irrigated by *seguias*. The new landowners quickly replaced the *seguias* with modern pipes that did not fulfil the same ecological service to the ecosystems. *Khetarras* also disappeared because of land mismanagement.

By highlighting the socioecological shortcomings of modern irrigation systems, researchers have raised the need to rehabilitate *khetarras*. During the COP22, in 2016, the Moroccan ministry of Agriculture, Aziz Akhannouch, presented the "Sustainable Oasis" initiative, based on the solidarity existing within the oasis as a model of resilience to Climate Change. Explaining that the initiative was based on Article 7 of the Paris Agreements (on the protection of most vulnerable ecosystems), he showed how it aimed to highlight the unique socioecological characters of oases, habitat of 28% of the world's population, and to value their heritage and help reinforce their resilient characteristics (ANDZOA, 2016). Talking more specifically about the ecological and social benefits brought by *khetarras*, Abdelatif Lahlou, member of the Association Meftah Essaad, pleaded in favour of the registration of these ancestral irrigation systems as UNESCO World Heritage, in view of helping to attract funding for their rehabilitation. He also warned of the serious ecological and economic and social damages the disappearance of the *khetarras* systems would entail (Groupe Archimedia, 2016).

Rethinking groundwater extraction

The modernization of water management system led to a strong reliance on more and more sophisticated technical means, some of which allowed to extract groundwater deeper and deeper. In the Moroccan society, a strange divide between groundwater users was observed: i.e., those in favour of digging deeper wells, using mechanized drilling methods, and those who, in the end, identified superior ecological benefits from keeping less-deep, traditionally built wells. Fofack et al. carried out a study in 2018 to document these choice-making processes. The farmers were split between those who used water dug from a traditional well and who lived in "a world of water-penury", and those who had decided to reach deeper waters thanks to mechanized drillings, who felt that they lived in "a world of water-abundance".

The construction of a well is manual. It involves the contribution of various types of labourers and specialists and is based on ancient and incremental know-how which has evolved over centuries and thus carries on being transferred. It also allows to share the responsibilities associated to the well. As Fofack et al. explain, for the well users, belonging to this community of labourers lies on a set of values and leads to a number of benefits. It allows them to learn how to deal with water-penury:

by becoming aware that the well water is not infinite and its quantity can be exhausted until the next ecological recharge. (…) They are acquiring their knowledge on how much time is needed to withdraw water, or on the time necessary for the well to be replenished, thanks to their practical experience.

(2018: 16)

Water digging techniques introduced new drilling tools, but also scientific expertise and skills. Syrian drillers, who arrived in the early 2000s, reduced drilling costs (that were previously beyond the reach of medium-sized operating farmers). However, they also very often proceeded without permits, and a real anarchism grew around access to groundwater and its overexploitation. The main competitors of the Syrian drillers, the Moroccan drilling companies, were encouraged to proceed by the Moroccan authorities who even urged farmers to use groundwater in order to counteract surface water shortages during the 1980s droughts.

The recent investigation carried out in the Saïss region showed that a significant number of boreholes had been dug between 2008 and 2014, based on the idea that they brought "water abundance" – the waters of the deep water table are captive and therefore flow with a greater pressure than groundwater which is "free". However, the research carried out by Fofack et al. (2018) has shown that, despite this, the use of old traditional wells is surviving, thanks to some water users who actively decided to disengage from the race for groundwater. This was because, in some cases, those who had attempted the transition to drilling were faced with failure: the drilling had not fulfilled its promises of abundance. In some others, the farmers realized how dependent on the world of drillers and its experts they had become. The return to the "world of scarcity", in this sense, was strangely reassuring because it is about a controlled scarcity accompanied by a social appropriation of the aquifer, which is robust and a guarantee of reliability. This shows that scarcity is a relative concept which must necessarily integrate, in order to be realistic, the adaptive capacities of societies and their needs.

The relatively recent realization that groundwater is being extremely overexploited has encouraged a return to a more sober approach to well management. Likewise, calls to decreasing water demand (instead of increasing water supply) open doors to new ways of thinking about scarcity, abundance, and modes of development. In the same way that the disqualification of certain practices, and the legitimization of others by the Basin Agencies, have influenced the choices of public opinion on the way in which aquifers should be exploited, the changing discourses on water governance and the enhancement of ecological interrelationships could begin to prove that the understanding of "traditional water fighters" on how to live with water scarcity could become useful to all.

Water conflicts: custodian practices versus new water laws

Many interesting studies have been carried out that focus on how legal changes related to water and land management have generated profound societal transformations in Morocco. One of them is of particular relevance in the context of this book. Paul Mathieu and his team (2001) described what happened when an external intervention (such as the introduction of a new irrigation technique or an institutional novelty such as the creation of new water users association) is introduced in a traditional community in Morocco. The objective was to observe who was learning from whom and how a consensus could be reached.

The introduction of an external system of irrigation inevitably disturbs traditional systems. Similarly, an external investment will change the distribution of water amongst users, their rights over the resource, and who has the authority to manage water issues and to negotiate water matters with the government. Mathieu et al. showed that, whilst in certain cases, external intervention will trigger negative, conflictual, or else passive response from the community affected by the intervention, in some other cases, a consensus can be reached where all parties at stake are involved and satisfied. Analysing conflictual situations can therefore help identify which factors and forms of social organization will facilitate the design of new institutional arrangements that conciliate traditional indigenous and external systems.

In line with this, Ahmed Benali (in Mathieu et al. 2001) explored the case of the rehabilitation of the great *seguia* Boulamaiz (located in the Rif region). This traditional irrigation system benefited from important repairs funded through an FAO project between 1989 and 1991. The rehabilitation work was accompanied by the creation of three agricultural water users associations designated to manage the water networks associated with the three irrigation canals.

Observing how the traditional and the new irrigation systems merged allowed Benali to draw the following conclusions. Before the rehabilitation of the *seguia*, two types of water users existed. The upstream owners of the "right to use water" had inherited the traditional custodian rights, since they belonged to the lineage of the founders of traditional irrigation systems. Owners of the water, they therefore managed it by following the principles of traditional water distribution in the community. Thus, upstream beneficiaries took it in turn to irrigate their fields, respecting the specific time and water pressure allocated to them. Farmers located downstream did not have similar water rights: their rights were not related to owning water but, rather, to using it. In the traditional irrigation system, they were allowed to use the entirety of the residual water coming from upstream – this was socially agreed within the community. During droughts, or when water was otherwise scarce, downstream farmers were given water by upstream owners, or exchanged water against labour. These actions were based on a strong solidarity within the community. They were also strongly linked to a respect for the "water authority" – trusted to be just and able to find an appropriate solution to each individual problem, hence made of good negotiators, capable to adapt.

In the case of Boulamaiz, this traditional system functioned perfectly well until 1994 – i.e., two years after the rehabilitation of the irrigation system and the creation of the Water Users Associations. The year 1994 brought a drought. It is believed that the water owners were not informed of the creation of the Water Users Association – or else they did not fully understand what was happening. This might well come from the fact that, since it seemed impossible to make more than 20% of water users in the community take part in the general meetings being organized by agricultural technicians, the administration decided to have the leaders of the associations elected. The water rights owners, confident that they had authority over water issues and generally disengaged with administrative interference, were left aside whilst the associations were effectively taking over their authority, following the new legal rights given to the Water Users Association. In practice, nothing really changed for two years.

However, when rain became rare in 1994, the water owners realized that the traditional system of "taking irrigation in turn" was not being respected anymore. A general assembly was organized to negotiate how the two irrigation management systems could possibly be linked. No consensus was found and the upstream water-rights owners (two-third of the water users on the land subjected to negotiation) decided to physically create a deviation for water to be reconnected to the old irrigation canal network. It is only after this, that people expressed a real wish to constructively identify ways to better manage their irrigation systems, taking account of both climatic and institutional constraints.

Agricultural local authorities agreed to give back certain distribution roles previously allocated to the water rights owners. They acknowledged traditional water rights and recognized the necessity to limit the volume of water used upstream so that the surplus resulting from the new irrigation system put into place by the government could be allocated downstream, whilst the upstream users' rights would carry on being respected. Besides, new leaders of the Water Users Association were elected, and the real authority over water rights and their application remains in the hands of the elderly water-rights owners of the community.

The lessons to be drawn are as follows. When the rehabilitation of the *seguia* started, there was an important gap in the way in which external investors and local stakeholders perceived the initiative. For the Moroccan administration and investors, once rehabilitated, the irrigation network of the *seguia* would represent one unified hydraulic entity, characterized by an upstream–downstream interdependency. For the water users, on the other hand, the sociohydrological territory had been traditionally defined completely differently and was based both on authority and solidarity. In the end, the external intervention triggered a reflection on how to best integrate new technological systems and traditional management systems to reach a sustainable consensus.

Water and agriculture

More and more researchers and official texts[1] are extending the ambition of protecting livelihoods through exploring the potential to preserve water heritage and linking it to agricultural heritage. Howard et al. (2008) worked on such a large-scale long-term programme aimed at scientifically conceptualizing GIAHS (Globally Important Agricultural Heritage Systems) as integrated social and ecological systems that are dynamically embedded in larger systems. The premise is that:

> an adequate scientific framework for the GIAHS Programme should help to reinforce the capacity of their stewards to sustain and enhance their lifeways and livelihoods, to safeguard against losses in biodiversity and ecosystem services and to allow for the continued evolution and adaptation of these systems.
>
> (2008, p. viii)

Many GIAHs have disappeared, and those that remain are under threat due to technological, economic, ecological, and cultural change drivers, which very often are related to government policies that actively seek to transform these systems, since their populations' resource base is perceived to be undeveloped. Change in these traditional systems has been especially quick, since the beginning of the XXth.

In the XXIst c., the pace of change has accelerated and the number of shocks and disturbances has increased, but new, more ecological ways of approaching development strategies are also being investigated, especially in times when globalization and non-ecological modes of productions have proved to have irreversible destructive effects on the planet. Identifying, prioritizing, and supporting traditional social–ecological systems could therefore be envisaged and understood as a global insurance policy and facilitate the emergence of agroecological principles which are urgently needed to develop more sustainable agroecosystems and agrobiodiversity conservation strategies both in industrial and developing countries. Support for GIAHS – estimated to cover 5 million hectares, and to support 2 billion people – will represent a reversal of centuries of policies that have both exploited and devalued such systems as well as disregarded the rights of indigenous peoples to maintain their lifeways (Howard et al. 2008).

In Morocco, the agricultural policy of the newly independent country completely disarticulated society by devaluing rural peasant ways of living. The rural world was very slow at embracing the output-focused logic advocated by the State. This became clear when it refused to cultivate certain new crops or when farmers occasionally damaged some agricultural equipment, as a sign of protest. As Pérennès (1993) stressed:

> the apparent failure of irrigated agriculture does not illustrate the incapacity of the rural community to modernise agricultural production but, rather, its social capacity to develop strategies to fight the growing control that the State is intending to impose on them using water infrastructure and modern management.
>
> (1993: 22)

It is regrettable that modern strategies didn't take account of rural communities' knowledge of how to cultivate soils whilst protecting their quality, how to use water in a sustainable way, how to survive numerous hazards such as droughts and poverty, and how to collectively build strategies that are beneficial to all through traditional forms of associations and village *Jmaas*. As Lazarev (2014) stressed, not only there is no doubt that the Moroccan rural world is alive and well, strong and innovative, but it is also very clear that the State's decision to not enable it to unfold and be empowered constitutes a missed opportunity.

Despite the State's reluctance to integrate peasant's know-how in agricultural strategies, some Moroccan researchers (from the Rabat Agronomical Institute) have examined how farmers developed resilient approaches during the 1980s drought. They then presented their findings, explaining the farmers' attitude to seeds conservation, timing for cultivation, and their capacity to deal with uncertainty and climatic irregularity, both in mountainous or in desert environment. Systemic reviews of indigenous agricultural practices and water management techniques were also carried by researchers of the Marseille Institute for Research and Development (Roose et al. 2010). One objective was to identify the know-how techniques used by rural communities and to ensure that these techniques could be better understood, better shared, and potentially adapted to other environments. The study was aimed at drawing useful lessons for the future of agriculture by helping to identify how new techniques of soil and water conservation developed by the IRD could be combined with traditional techniques still used in agriculture in small subsistence farms. Their study led to the identification of high-potential zones where modern techniques of soil and water conservation could be combined with traditional approaches, taking account of the status of land, the choices made by the local community and the possibility to mobilize labourers. One major constraint was to support younger people by showing to them the possibilities to find long-term solutions that would stop them from having to leave the countryside to find jobs in the city. Both adaptations of existing agricultural methods in varied natural environments and suggestions to improve agricultural techniques were examined (Roose et al. 2010: 214, 298).

By combining traditional approaches with more modern ecological agronomic methods shared throughout North Africa, one important idea was to create a new perception of "modernity" in the rural world, one that would be empowering to the local communities who could be in charge of agricultural practices opted for, and combine them with more traditional ones. This could genuinely give hope to the rural world for the future.

Following this line of thoughts, one agricultural approach that is being revisited – because its principles seem very close to a sustainable approach of water, soil, and rural community management – is that of the "Agdal". Auclair (2012: 25) described it as a *"community heritage that can help people to face the insecurity linked to natural resources usage and to build socio-ecological resilience and adaptability"*. Whilst Auclair and his colleagues focused specifically on the study of the High Atlas pastoral agdals, El Faiz (2015), motivated by Professor Abdelaziz Balal, thoroughly reexamined the lessons given by the Arabo-muslim agronomy treaties on oasis and non-irrigated agriculture, in view of developing alternative development approaches to "participatory heritage conservation" and to attempt to reintegrate oral modes of transmission and training amongst modern agricultural communities. The studies go on.

Conclusion

Is traditional knowledge necessarily attached to the past or could it be appropriate in a current context and help to find solutions to current constraints? For the IISD:

> traditional knowledge is information, skills, practices and products – often associated with indigenous peoples – which is acquired, practiced, enriched and passed on through generations. It is typically deeply rooted in a specific political, cultural, religious and environmental context, and is a key part of the community's interaction with the natural environment.
>
> (IISD, 2003: 5)

A priori, there is no implication that these technologies could not help meet communities' needs in a current setting. However, societal transformations have led to the fact that there are fewer skilled people who know these traditional systems and who can maintain them. In addition, populations haven't suffered the real cost incurred by the introduction of modern technologies (for instance electric-powered tube wells) since the government heavily subsidised such investments. As Adeel et al. (2008) stressed, *"using 'real cost pricing' methodologies in the context of water-as-a-human-right debate allows to highlight the fact that new water management approaches do not compare favourably against more traditional ones when all the costs are accounted for"* (Adeel et al. 2008: 7).

Adapting traditional techniques to a new societal and technological context corresponds to a real cultural type of innovation. By exploring a few practical examples, this chapter illustrated the fact that not only this type of innovation is necessary, but it is also possible. It is thanks to better water governance, an issue explored in the next chapter, that stakeholders will be able to share knowledge and ideas on how to enable this best.

Note

1 Agenda 21 (recognizes rural peoples as major stewards of natural resources); Paragraph 40 of the Johannesburg Declaration on Sustainable Development (promotes "the conservation, sustainable use, and management of traditional and indigenous models of agricultural production"); Article 8 of the Convention on Biological Diversity (includes the mandate to "respect, preserve, and maintain knowledge, innovations and practices of indigenous and local communities embodying traditional lifestyles"), to quote a few.

References

Adeel, Z., B. Schuster and H. Bigas (2008) *What Makes Traditional Technologies Tick?* Ontario: United Nations University, INWEH.

Agence Nationale pour le Développement des Zones Oasiennes et de l'Arganier (ANDZOA) (2016) http://andzoa.ma/fr/2016/11/15/cop22-presentation-de-linitiative-oasis-durables-par-m-le-ministre-de-lagriculture/, accessed on 28th of September 2020.

Auclair, L. (2012) Un patrimoine socio-écologique a l'épreuve des transformations du monde rural. In Auclair, L. and Alifriqui, M. (Eds.) *Agdal. Patrimoine socio-écologique de l'Atlas marocain.* Rabat: Institut Royal de la culture Amazighe et IRD, El Maarif éditions. pp. 23–71.

El Alaoui, M. (2004) Les pratiques participatives des associations d'usagers de l'eau dans la gestion de l'irrigation au Maroc; étude de cas en petite, moyenne et grande hydraulique. In Hammami, A., Kuper, M. and Debbarh A. (Eds.) *La modernisation de l'agriculture irriguée,* tome 2 – Actes du séminaire euro-méditerranéen. Rabat: Projet INCO-WADEMED: pp. 146–163.

El Faiz, M. (2001) La Grande Hydraulique dans le Haouz de Marrakech. In Ben Sedrine, S. and Gobe, E. (Ed.) *Les ingénieurs maghrébins et les systèmes de formations.* Tunis: IRMC, pp. 213–225.

El Faiz, M. (2015) *Agronomie et agronomes d'Al Andalous (XI –XIVe s.).* Casablanca: La croisée des chemins.

El Faiz, M. and T. Ruf (2007) *La gestion collective de l'eau est-elle encore possible dans le Nfis à l'ouest de Marrakech?* http://hal.cirad.fr/cirad-00154399, accessed on 19th October 2020.

Fofack, R. et al. (2018) Analyse du basculement des modes d'extraction des eaux souterraines dans le Saiss (Maroc). *Journal du Développement durable et territoires,* 9 (2). http://journals.openedition.org/developpementdurable/12197, accessed on 19th of October 2020.

Groupe Archimedia (2016) Pour la sauvegarde des khetarras au Maroc. *Chantiers du Maroc* N. 145. www.construction21.org/france/articles/fr/pour-la-sauvegarde-des-khettaras-au-maroc.html, accessed on 28th of September 2020.

Howard, P, Puri, R, Smith, L, and Altierri, M. (2008) *A Scientific Conceptual Framework and Strategic Principles for the Globally Important Agricultural Heritage Systems Programme from a Social-Ecological Systems Perspective.* Rome: FAO.

IISD (2003) *Traditional Knowledge and Patentability. IISD Trade and Development Brief N. 7.* Winnipeg: International Institute for Sustainable Development.

Lazarev, G. (2014) *Ruralité et changement social. Etudes sociologiques.* Université Mohamed V Agdal. Série Essais et Etudes N. 64. Rabat: Editions Bouregreg.

Lightfoot, D.R. (1996) Moroccan khetara: traditional irrigation and progressive desiccation. *Geoforum.* 27 (2): 261–273.

Mathieu, P., A. Benali and O. Aubriot (2001) Dynamiques institutionnelles et conflit autour des droits d'eau dans un système d'irrigation traditionnel au

Maroc. *Revue Tiers Monde* 42 (166): 353–374. https://hal.archives-ouvertes. fr/hal-00595983, accessed on 19th of October 2020.

Pérennès, J. (1993) *L'eau et les hommes au Maghreb. Contribution à une politique de l'eau en Méditerranée.* Paris: Karthala.

Roose, E., M. Sabir and A. Laouina (2010) *Gestion durable de l'eau et des sols au Maroc. Valorisation des techniques traditionnelles méditerranéennes.* Marseille: IRD.

7 Towards new forms of water governance

Decentralization and actors of the Moroccan water sector

Water management stakeholders

In order to have a better understanding of what improving water governance entails, it is important to remind ourselves of who water actors currently are in Morocco. According to Al-Alaween et al. *"they can be categorized into four distinct levels: main advisory, executive, public and private operators, and local water users These can be subdivided into three main groups: consultative and coordination, ministry departments, and public institutions plus water users"* (2016: 22).

The complexity of this structure of stakeholders and governance somehow reflects that of the water physical environment and patterns of use. Whilst the Ministry of Land Management, Water and the Environment (MATEE) is, in principle, the main water actor (Tazi Sadeq, 2006), in practice the Ministry of Finance has the largest power over public establishments and local authorities.

Other ministries (e.g., the Ministry of Interior and the Ministry of Agriculture and Marine Fisheries), important overarching institutions (e.g., the Inter-Ministerial Water Commission and the Higher Council for Water and Climate), more regional, or local administrations (e.g., the Regional Councils of the Environment, local authorities, and prefectural assemblies) and around 30 major water operators working in water production and distribution for drinking purposes and irrigation, all account as "water stakeholders" in Morocco. The distribution of drinking water is ensured either by the National Office of Electricity and Water (ONEE), the leading producer of drinking water, or by concession to a private operator.

Despite this complexity and the plethora of actors supposedly involved, the communication between stakeholders remains weak and some of the institutions actually only convened once since their creation (it is for instance the case for the Inter-Ministerial Water Commission and the Higher Council for Water and Climate who, since 2001, has been inactive).

In the 1990s, Morocco's water sector underwent significant reorganization when nine River Basin Agencies (RBAs) were set up to regulate the water sector in each of the country's river basins. The governance of water was therefore going "territorial" – geographically cut into basins (although, culturally, not necessarily fitting the Amazigh tribes living in different parts of Morocco). In order to contextualize our understanding of what the RBAs were about to be asked to do, we first need to explain the notion of land management (*Aménagement du Territoire – AdT*) and the advanced regionalization project in Morocco.

Land management and the advanced regionalization project

The management shift from "water from the sky" to "water from the State" was not immediately accompanied by an overall political vision and plan on how to manage the water resources of the Moroccan territory. However, land management had already been on the agenda (albeit mainly through the objective of land speculation and agrarian capitalism purposes) and a "Ministère de l'Habitat et de l'Aménagement du Territoire" had even been created. Originally, the new philosophy behind land management (AdT) brought new concepts based on the dominance of the city as an economic catalyst. Then, in 2007, the concept of sustainable territorial development emerged and extended AdT to the whole territory. Three years later, the creation of 16 regions came out of the "advanced regionalization" project, aimed at ensuring a coordinated and concerted type of territorial management, through a new type of stakeholder: the regional collectivity, privileged partner of the State – in charge of integrating all regional plans whilst respecting the legal autonomy and skills specific to the region.

Two types of regions were created: those centred on economically growing cities and the non-polarized ones, covering mountainous areas, deserts, and oases in need of support in terms of national solidarity. The ambitious plan, as described in the Rapport sur la *régionalisation avancée* (CCR, 2011), is:

> planned around a progressive decentralisation, an enforced democratisation, an acceleration of development, a socio-politico and administrative modernisation of the country and good governance. (…) For the State, as well as for citizens, at all levels, this project is

to become a philosophical, historical and practical reference in the sort-run and for generations to come.

(2011: p. 5)

As Houria Tazi Sadeq showed (2006), water plays a crucial role in AdT in Morocco. She explained that:

> the integration between the environmental, economic and social domains within AdT has been perceived as a progress. So much that the national debate on AdT organised from 1999 showed that water is a structuring component of land management through AdT.

(2006: p. 133)

Thinking in terms of AdT pushed the State to encourage the creation of new institutions. Thus, following the new 1995 Water Law, the Interministerial Commission for Water was created in 2001. Following the same logic, local Commissions were given the role to operationalize sustainable water management at the local level.

Whilst the success of the advanced regionalization should be measured by the effectiveness of such local institutions, observing how these local commissions operate gives a worrying picture of what "advanced regionalization" really means in democratical terms. Half of the members of these commission are members of the State and of public institutions. The other half includes the president of the local commission, the president of the agricultural and industrial chamber, three designated (not elected) people who represent local communities, and one person representing ethnic communities. It is clear that, for now, the central power remains dominant. Creating new local institutions is clearly not enough to genuinely facilitate local participation in action and in decision-making.

Local water stakeholders and advanced regionalization

One of the main objectives of advanced regionalization project is to decentralize management and to ensure that regional plans are being carried out in coordination and coherence with national plans.

Thus, at local levels, the numerous national stakeholders (ministries and interministerial institutions, notably) are represented in various ways. For instance, the Ministry of agriculture, rural development and fisheries controls nine Regional Organisations (ORMVAs) in charge of putting into practice the ministry's strategy of irrigation equipment, water regional management, framers' training, water policing, and maintenance of water equipment. Their operating costs are derived from the selling of water – not a good incentive for them to encourage the reduction of water consumption. Farmers' participation in decision-making processes is minimal. Similarly, the Interior Ministry is represented locally by water companies – who provide drinking water and deal with sanitation issues in rural and urban zones – as well as by dispatched authorities (regional governors and wallis – local police). The ("diluted") presence of the State is never too far.

One of the most important examples of water stakeholder at the local level is that of the River Basin Agencies, representing MATEE on the ground. One main novelty in the concept of RBA is to work beyond the administrative organization of the territory in order to, instead, respect the ecological boundaries of the actual river basins. Following this principle, there are therefore nine RBA in Morocco. They translate, through the principles of AdT, issues related to the natural environment, in view of facilitating the global management, decentralized and integrated of these issues at the national level.

Financially equipped, they can provide financial and technical help as well as put into place some water infrastructures to protect communities from floods, carry out quantitative and qualitative measurements related to water, and deliver authorizations for water usage. They keep an overall track of how measures on the ground respect the national integrated plan for water resources management, as well as of initiatives undertaken and authorisations given.

The functioning of the RBAs has been questioned and there is still considerable room for improvement. Al Alaween et al. (2016: 24), in particular, have explored a series of important shortcomings. First, they explained that the RBAs were given vast responsibilities under the 1995 water law without the necessary funding and structures to carry out their regulatory mandate. Second, whilst the division of responsibility for enforcement between the RBAs and MoI is unclear, internally there are also issues with the way tenders are written, leading at times to favouritism in the tendering process. This considerably reduces the credibility of the RBAs. "*Some private sector firms have also noted the presence of unlicensed firms in the water sector that neither pay taxes nor treat their employees within the confines of the law*" (Al Alaween et al. 2016: 24).

The authors also showed that, in terms of budgeting, the implementation of the Green Morocco Plan is being carried out with a complete lack of transparency. This main agricultural strategy aimed at modernizing agriculture and at providing subsidies and grants to small farmers, was not developed in coordination with the RBAs or the delegated ministry responsible for water. As a result, *"the subsidies are not reaching small farmers, many of whom have to face a labyrinth of regulations they do not understand in order to secure this aid. They therefore see the program-me as non-transparent"* (Al Alaween, 2016: 24). There is therefore an integrity risk attached to the way in which the RBAs conduct their affairs on the ground, with repeated practices of favouritism and preferential arrangements with associates.

Despite strong criticisms concerning the ways in which water stakeholders have been given authorities on the ground, one has to recognize that many efforts are put into improving transparency and participation. Other local stakeholders, including less official ones, are taking more initiatives. In the water sector, cooperation, associations, and partnership initiatives have been observed. Houria Tazi Sadeq (2006) mentions, in particular, the PAGER program, aimed at ensuring the participation of all stakeholders involved in agricultural projects, from the decision-making phase to the maintenance one, to guaranty the sustainability of the projects. Another example is the strengthening of associations and Water Users Associations, following the Dahir (law) n1-87. Even more importantly, thousands of rural associations and NGOs, in direct contact with local communities in urban and rural settings, are becoming much more active at all levels. Environmental NGOs such as the AMED Association Marocaine pour un Développement Durable,[1] or the AMEPN Association Marocaine pour l'Ecotourisme et la Protection de la Nature,[2] help to raise citizens' awareness on the interconnectedness of environmental and developmental issues.

Despite the creation of new local institutions, participation, empowerment, and the capacity to take initiatives need to progressively be strengthened if water governance is to improve. This will entail a better understanding of why water matters in sustainable development, why environmental information needs to be better shared and how communication should be improved. It is on these points that the next section focuses.

The relevance of water issues in public debates

Improved governance goes beyond the creation of new institutions and laws: a whole change of paradigm and mentality, that would include trust and empowerment, needs to emerge. There is a long way to go for this to happen.

Taking the example of rising environmental problems and the fragility of environmental governance in North Africa, Malka (2018: 3) explained that:

> In 2017, water shortages precipitated a series of occasionally violent protests in Morocco. In the Rif region, protesters demanded that the government take action against local growers who were overusing water for water-intensive cannabis production. Activists in the Beni Mellal region decried the high cost of water access (...). Moroccans in several towns demonstrated about the lack of clean drinking water. In Zagora, which has struggled with water access for decades, 23 people were arrested after clashes with police.

Other authors (Houdret et al. 2018: 2) concluded that "*Policy-makers need to be more aware of the links between environmental governance and its potential impact on human rights and political stability*".

Working at improving water governance would therefore not only help understand better how to meet people's needs, help the economy of the country but it would also ensure that strategies are constructed, shared, and embraced by and for the benefit of all.

The rise of a hydropolitical awareness

Requiring the participation of citizens in water matters implies that people are considered as citizens in the first place. With regards to water issues in Morocco, tensions rose when people started being considered mainly as clients and water resources as commodities. From this, a hydropolitical awareness emerged. Gradually, the poorest Moroccan communities learnt how to express their dissatisfaction. It was a water problem that had prompted them, back in 1929, to organize protests against the difficult access to water resources and the lack of work. As Pennel (2003) underlines, it was in this tense climate that the French Protectorate had decided to legally interfere on collective Berber land. By creating the *Dahir Berbère* in 1930, they wanted to separate customary Berber laws from the Muslim *Shari'a* system, hence separating the communities. Moroccans had reacted against it, unified in a nationalist movement.

More recently, one of the reasons that motivated the water-related uprising has been the commodification of water. However, the problem most raised by the demonstrators is not so much related to varying water prices: more importantly, people are shocked by the domination of the private sector, the State's abandonment of its primary obligations in terms of water management, and the lack of governance concerning the management of this vital resource. Mehdi Lahlou and his team from ACME (Association for a Global Water Contract) (Lahlou, 2010) explain that:

> since the mid-1990s, a tendency towards greater deregulation, privatization and opening up to large foreign capital has been observed. Private capital has strengthened its presence in fundamental sectors such as education and health, under the pretext that the State no longer has the means to meet the financial needs of these sectors.

From then on, nothing would stop the State from addressing water shortages and water distribution through market forces mainly. The logic: (a) water is vital but scarce, and the market knows how to manage scarcity; (b) public authorities of southern countries are not able to guarantee efficient macroeconomic management. It is this logic that international financial institutions (WB and IMF in particular) advised governments of southern countries to adopt, especially in the 1980s. And, it is precisely this same logic that has been followed by the Moroccan authorities until now.

However, times are changing and, at the start of the XXIst c., many voices are being raised, even in European countries (particularly in France), to call for the remunicipalization of water management in order to defend the right to water for all. The objective is to ensure that water "*is once again considered as a public good in essence, of which the community cannot cede production, preservation, distribution and management to the market*" (El Menouar, 2012: 87).

Weak legal settings for participatory processes to take place

The observed rise in a hydropolitical awareness has occasionally been fuelled by weak legal settings, or the weak implementations of laws when these are already in place. Houdret et al. (2018) carried out interviews with local stakeholders in a project called STRIPE (Strengthening the Right to Information for People and the Environment). They concluded that:

> there is a significant gap between strong legal foundations and their implementation. Recent frameworks such as the new constitutions are ambitious, but the implementation of sector-based strategies, regulatory and disclosure mechanisms, together with the

institutional framework, are still far from securing transparent and accountable environmental governance.

(2018: 5)

Generally speaking, the will to see citizens participate more contrasts with the lack of recognition of some of their rights. One practical case study caught the attention of the public when, with the help of the Democratic Association of Moroccan Women (ADFM), a women's movement called "Soulaliyate" fought for their rights over land ownership and compensation when they were displaced, following the rent or sale of the collective land they were living and working on. In contrast to the men, the women did not benefit from indemnities: struggling for justice, they now demand equal rights to avoid ending up in poverty. The Soulaliyate movement carries on strengthening women's knowledge about their social and economic rights. They help them to formulate their complaints and provide platforms to elaborate new regulations. Other examples of citizens fighting for their water rights are now multiplying.[3]

Al Alaween et al. (2016) stressed that remaining risks to integrity include unsettled and disputed tribal claims on water sources, in which the State is opposed to traditional users. As they explained, *"while there is an on-going national conversation about land titles, the same conversation has not yet taken place about water rights"* (2016: 14). Besides, it is important to stress that the 1995 water law did not address traditional uses of water at all and that stakeholders were not fully consulted in its making. The relationship between the current law and tribal and communal rights is not resolved.

Lack of environmental information

Being hydropolitically aware, or knowing your (water) rights implies that information is generated and circulates. In Morocco, there is a very strong tradition of oral transmission of the information. However nowadays, information circulates differently – if it does. Part of current weaknesses in governance are linked to shortcomings in keeping citizens informed.

This right to access information in order to be able to actively take part in the decision-making process is core to the Universal Declaration of Human rights and other international frameworks such as the Rio Declaration and the Aarhus Convention. The latter, which *"enables citizens to seek justice in cases where the human right to live in an adequate, safe and healthy environment has been violated, hasn't been ratified by Morocco so far"* (Houdret et al., 2018: 2). The 2011 Arab Spring increased people's awareness of their lack of political participation and the civil society's readiness to complain about the negative impacts of bad environmental governance is high. Claims for effective access to information are among their key demands. The 2011 Moroccan Constitution responded to these requests by promising more inclusive governance as well as transparent decision-making and by promising equal rights to access to water (Malka, 2018).

In addition, a new improved water law (Law 36-15) has focused on improving water information systems and establishing better connection between water institutions (El Menouar, 2012). The implementation of the Sustainable Development Goals (SDGs) may also provide new opportunities for action, with Goal 16 being focused on the importance of inclusive decision-making and access to information. However, in many cases, the implementation of new laws and the respect of new initiatives such as implementing the SDGs, is indeed very slow.

In a civil society public opinion survey, Houdret et al. identified that *"58% of Moroccans felt that more tools and resources were needed to help the general public understand their right to access information and only 9% of them felt people have opportunities to participate in environmental pollution decision-making"* (2018: 3). It is often a lack of information that leads to conflicts. Thus, for instance, when local inhabitants of Ben Smim realized that a private investor was about to start constructing a plant for bottled water in their village whilst they hadn't been informed, they protested and ended up blocking the construction site to avoid the water supply for their households and livestock being cut off. Later, the plant nevertheless opened but did not respect the volume quota that had been agreed. The dissemination of information about their bad practice, thanks to sympathetic journalists, helped the story reached the headlines and people become more sensitive to the impact that hidden information can have on their livelihood.

As a consequence, efforts are being put into addressing the issue of environmental information. It is clear that in environmental ministries' websites, basic information on environmental planning and monitoring is either outdated or not available. Besides, *"the Adaptation Finance Accountability Initiative (AFAI) has called for improved access to information about climate-finance processes to avoid the misappropriation of funds and ensure more targeted and sustainable adaptation planning"* (Houdret et al., 2018: 3). The call for improvement of information provision and quality, in view of fighting corruption, has been addressed in a plethora of ways (e.g., creation of institutions such as the Central Authority for Corruption Prevention (CACP) in 2007; 40 measures put into place by the government to fight corruption and increase transparency in 2010; anti-corruption campaigns involving the media and civil society in 2012, use of ICTs – web portal to report abuses and e-government tools, etc.). Nevertheless, *"despite these efforts, resources lost to corruption is sufficient to fund the entire Moroccan military"* (Al Alaween et al., 2016: 23).

Shortcomings in communication

Access to environmental information not only means that information is being gathered and made available; people also need to understand what it means. Communicated in scientific terms, or through concepts, messages related to water problems or strategies will be meaningless to a large portion of the Moroccan population who is still illiterate (32%) or, if educated, unwilling to be tricked by jargon. Other communication problems will carry on jeopardizing progresses in water governance. As Al Aaween et al. (2016: 24) have stressed, *"administrators tasked with water management often use French but their constituency is more often than not Arabic and Tamazight speaking"*. There are also cultural gaps within a same country that do not help communication with, for instance, River Basin Agencies personnel lacking the social dimension to address populations and their needs.

Failure in communication can also simply result from understanding water issues at stake entirely differently. In practice, this is almost systematically the case with rural communities and officials not understanding each other's perspective and objective.

Auclair and Alfriqui (2012) extensively described this paradigm gap when explaining how, in the Agdal agricultural practices, ecological dimensions are closely related to socioeconomic ones. The legal status of collective land is defined in relation to the need to adapt to the natural environment and makes land a natural–cultural heritage, as opposed a set of natural resources to be used for economic purposes. In more theoretical terms, Boelens et al. (2016: 3) described this through the notion of "hydrosocial territories", the construction of which *"needs to be analyzed in the context of their historical, cultural and political settings (…) and simultaneously embody the natural and the social; the biophysical and the cultural; the hydrological and the hydraulic; the material and the political"*. Water governance is therefore intimately linked to what the authors call "territorial politics". The latter *"finds expression in encounters of diverse actors - with divergent spatial and political-geographical interests – whose territory-building projections and strategies compete, superimpose and align to strengthen specific water-control claims*". This is truly a communication issue as "*territorial struggles go beyond battles over natural resources, involving struggles over meaning, norms, knowledge, identity, authority and discourses*" (Boelens et al., 2016: 1).

Effectively, if water governance is to be improved in Morocco, the variety of stakeholders are going to have to open up to each other's perspectives on how human communities can facilitate the generation of life through using water most appropriately and sustainably.

Conclusion

Behind the notion of water governance, as this chapter has shown, lies the complexity of the water sector in terms of stakeholders, the slow changes in legal documents and their lack of implementation, but also, generally, the lack of reliant information on water issues, and modes of communication that still need considerable improvement.

An improved type of water governance in Morocco is very much needed. Not only to address the injustice and inequalities that exist regarding water distribution, rights, and pricing, but also to generate new modes of communication, learning, and participatory decision-making processes that can help in creating better, more sustainable water strategies. Water stakeholders need to both express themselves and find a new place and role in new governance settings, using new modes of communication. What is for sure is that, despite the mirage given by the technology-centred modern approaches, water problems, and their solutions are not politically neutral, managerial issues, that can be objectively solved. As Malka (2018: 1) stressed, "*access to clean water is not only vital to sustain life; it has also become a key government function and powerful symbol of state legitimacy*" and "*unless growth strategies are accompanied by more effective water management strategies, these plans threaten to exacerbate the Maghreb's water stress, fuel more social unrest, and deepen inequalities*".

There is room for hope as debates on water issues are multiplying,[4] as well as numerous NGO initiatives, showing that "action is louder than words".[5] Hence, the general public's participation is not reduced to protests born out of desperation and injustice.

Notes

1 www.amedurable
2 https://amepn.ma/2020/03/24/https:-amepn-activites/

3 For example, a community of Amazigh people is struggling with the access to and pollution of their water reserves since the Imider silver mine has been established. They have peacefully protested to ensure their ability to remain in their homes and to restore the khettara system damaged by the mine – https://minorityrights.org/morocco-an-amazigh-communitys-long-wait-for-water-rights/, accessed on 13th of October 2020.

4 For example, Festival des musiques sacrées: Forum sur l'eau (Fondation Esprit de Fès, 2017).

5 Dodson and Bargach (2015) described a local NGO initiative to capture water (fog) through a system of nets, on the southern coast of Morocco. Another example is that of KAS-REMENA, an international NGO which promotes cooperation among MENA countries and with the EU. Active in Morocco, it has launched a training program to engage in in-depth reporting on urgent water and sanitation matters. www.moroccoworldnews.com/2020/06/304998/water-and-sanitation-ngo-cewas-to-launch-mena-water-journalism-training/

References

Al-Alaween, M., Jacobson, M., Jaraiseh, A., and Weinberg, J. (Eds.) (2016) Water Integrity in the Middle East and North Africa Region: Synthesis Report of Water Integrity Risks Assessments in Jordan, Lebanon, Morocco, Palestine and Tunisia. Stockholm: UNDP Water Governance Facility at SIWI.

Auclair, L. and M. Alifriqui (Eds.) (2012) *Agdal. Patrimoine socio-écologique de l'Atlas marocain.* Rabat: Institut Royal de la culture Amazighe et IRD, El Maarif éditions.

Boelens, R., J. Hoogesteger, E. Swyngedouw, J. Vos and P. Wester (2016) Hydrosocial territories: a political ecology perspective, *Water International.* 41 (1): 1–14. http://dx.doi.org/10.1080/02508060.2016.1134898, accessed on 05th of October 2020.

Commission Consultative de la Régionalisation (2011) *Rapport sur la régionalisation avancée.* Rabat: Royaume du Maroc.

Dodson, L.L. and J. Bargach (2015) *Harvesting fresh water from fog in rural Morocco, Procedia Engineering* 107: 186–193. http://creativecommons.org/licences/by-nc-nd/4.0/, accessed on 07th of October 2020.

El Menouar, A. (2012) *Pour une gouvernance optimale de l'eau au Maroc.* Rabat: Imprimerie Bidadaoui.

Fondation Esprit de Fès (2017) *Forum 2017. L'eau et le sacré.* Fès: Les éditions de la fondation Esprit de Fès.

Houdret, A., I. Pasqua and S. Meknassi Filali (2018) Access to environmental information: a driver of accountable governance in Morocco and Tunisia? *Briefing Paper 10/2018.* Bonn: Deutsches Institut für Entwicklungspolitik (DIE). http://dx.doi.org/10.23661/bp10.2018, accessed on 15th of October 2020.

Lahlou, M. (2010) La privatisation de l'eau au Maroc: premiers constats à partir de l'expérience de la Lyonnaise des Eaux à Casa, in *Partage des Eaux*. www. partagedeseaux.info/La-privatisation-de-l-eau-au-Maroc-premiers-constats-a-partir-de-l-experience

Malka, H. (2018) *Water, Protest and State Legitimacy in the Maghreb. Analysis Paper June*, 8 pages. Washington, DC: Centre for Strategic and International Studies CSIS, https://csis-website-prod.s3.amazonaws.com/s3fs-public/publication/181207_Maghreb_water_paper.pdf, accessed on 13th of October 2020.

Pennel, C.R. (2003) *Morocco. From Empire to Independence.* Oxford: Oneworld Book.

Tazi Sadeq, H. (2006) *Du droit de l'eau au droit à l'eau au Maroc et ailleurs.* Casablanca: La croisée des chemins.

Conclusion
Reviving practices, revaluing people

The disastrous effects of climate change in North Africa, the social movements observed there since the Arab Spring in 2011, but also the ways in which globalization is currently being reassessed, in particular with regards to food security, as a result of the Covid-19 pandemic, are all raising questions concerning the type of economic development that could help build resilience and, within it, the core role of water management in arid and semi-arid areas.

Through a historical perspective, this book has retraced the evolution of "water management practices" in Morocco and has highlighted how central it was to economic development, in particular through its agricultural policies.

It seems that, in various parts of the world, a paradigmic shift is emerging that is questioning economic market-centred values whilst paying more attention to ecological–economic links, as well as to ways in which our activities could – if changed – help us to become more resilient. Within this set of debates and reflexion, studies on indigenous practices, rights and know-how are finding their place as well as more opportunities to be communicated and listened to. As knowledge evolves on how to improve the management of natural resources, echoes are being found in traditional water management practices; advanced scientific findings can, at times, reconnect with knowledge which was sometimes developed centuries before. This is the case with the lessons drawn by the agronomists of Al-Andalous who, whilst bringing their know-how from vibrant civilizations in the Middle East into Moorish Europe, were facilitating the integration of cultures, religions, and ways of living both in cities and within water-scarce natural surroundings. New advanced in agroecology, ecological justice, and complex adaptive management extensively relate to old agronomic practices in subsistence agriculture, which knew how to use the natural environment whilst enriching and restoring it.

Whilst North African communities are often described as remarkable water-civilizations, their glorious hydraulic heritage has, for long, remained unknown or else ignored, or even pushed aside by the governments that are currently in place. It is clear that history has broken the ties with an intimate ecological–economic knowledge on how to work with the natural environment in order to meet communities' needs through a set of know-how practices that has best been developed by "people of the land", indigenous people. This book explored how modern economic practices, through three main strains (economic, technological, and governance-centred), have attempted to redesign an understanding of economic strategies, and how to create well-being in an independent country that exchanges and communicates with the rest of the world through trade and migration.

This book is not intended to draw a list of economic successes and failures of Morocco. Rather, it is an attempt to illustrate, through the specific example of water management, how opting for a certain type of modernity has led to water crises of economic, ecological as well as sociopolitical dimensions.

Part I highlighted a certain unity amongst indigenous people of North Africa, the Berbers. Originally nomadic people, having travelled from Eastern Europe and the Middle East, they settled in North African regions and learnt how to move their animals to different lands, depending on the seasons and the availability of water. They also learnt how to use water and different types of soil, in order to grow various types of crops. Their know-how was influenced by various civilizations (Roman, Greek, Nabatean, Byzantine), one of which, the Arab one, had a particular importance, in that it introduced particularly ingenious agronomical techniques. Now firmly identifying themselves as "Moroccans", the Berbers of the most Western part of North Africa have nevertheless not been fully integrated in the governance of the country and in the decision-making processes. Their culture was dominated by the pan-Arabism movement of the post-independence era, and it is only thanks to the revival of the Berber movement, much later in the XXth c., that the Amazigh culture regained recognition and an official voice. How much that voice is being listened to, and to what extent it can count in strategic decision-making, is debatable. What is for sure is that water stress and problems arising from the mismanagement of water shortages have recently generated enough social tension for subgroups of people within the Berber movement (those more interested in marginalized and impoverished rural areas) to raise their voice again. Recognizing the value of Berber culture should not be reduced to considering it as a "folkloric add-on": it is time for indigenous knowledge on ecological practices, as well as environmental governance, to be explored and shared, and introduced in the changing policies of the country. This is particularly true at a time when the government intends to encourage an advanced type of regionalization which, through increased decentralization, is intended to encourage more local participation.

In Part II, we explored a history of "modern water management" in Morocco, from the XIXth c., when forms of agrarian capitalism developed, all the way until now, via the French Protectorate (1912–1956) and the post-independence "modern times". The first chapter showed how international exchanges (commerce) and land management changes transformed the hierarchical structure in the Moroccan society, and how these changes facilitated the creation of the French Protectorate. The way in which water resources became "controlled" – by the construction of new infrastructures such as dams, through the creation of new legal systems, and a focus on priority activities, mainly agriculture – was then examined in view of explaining the dynamic of marginalization and disempowerment of rural communities. In the second chapter, the various dimensions of modernity were presented. The focus on technology and infrastructure projects (large dams, water transfers, large-scale irrigation techniques, etc.) transformed agricultural activities and focalized them in certain areas of the country, responding to certain economic priorities, such as agricultural exports. The technological transformation of agriculture had direct social impacts, in that smaller farmers in rural areas got detached from the main activities. The modernization of the governance system reinforced geographical – and cultural – disparities, and various shortcomings emerged from modernization strategies. These included increased water scarcity (with an overexploitation of groundwater resources and too high an economic focus on thirsty crops for exports); weaknesses in technological fixes (siltation and evaporation in dams, lack of maintenance of large infrastructures, illegal water drilling, insufficient waste water treatment in cities – to quote a few); and unfair governance (with unaffordable water prices being imposed to most vulnerable communities, and clashes between new water laws and stakeholders and traditional custodian settings). The outcomes of the modernization of water management call for new approaches.

Part III attempted to focus on such alternative approaches. It did so in three ways. First, by describing how people are exploring alternative approaches to "economic development". Primarily constraint by a rapidly growing water stress, population and urbanization, the government is well aware of the fact that mismanaging water could lead to social unrest because water is the core of any activity, of any life. Whilst scientific domains considered as "forward-looking" – such as complex adaptive management, agroecology, or ecological economics – are unfolding in research active areas of the world (USA, Canada, agronomical centres such as the French IRD, etc.), they are identifying useful lessons to be drawn from indigenous practices around the world. The cooperation and collaboration between very new and very traditional approaches is effectively generating a "new take on modernity", totally different from what we understood about modernity so far. Alternative development approaches in Morocco could open up to these approaches – and are doing so, although very timidly. Some projects, focused on alternative technologies and approaches in Morocco, are presented in the second chapter of that part. They talk of the rehabilitation of old irrigation systems, soil conservation, and agronomy techniques, groundwater exploitation, and water conflict management. Ultimately, introducing a new approach to water management that is more respectful of the natural environment will have to show more respect towards communities of the rural world too. This is what the third chapter, focused on water governance, shows. Whilst a massive project of "advanced regionalization", aimed at enhancing participation at the local level, is underway, a plethora of new water stakeholders are being created that do not necessarily cooperate, that are not all necessarily active and who, ultimately, refer to central authority. New governance initiatives are constantly slowed down by measures that will ensure that, despite good will, governance is kept centralized. In the background, a fundamental lack of information (both in terms of its generation, its circulation, and its credibility) and of communication (lack of transparency and differences in languages and paradigms that stop people from understanding each other) constitute a major weakness of the water governance system. However, the rise of a hydropolitical awareness is unofficially addressing these issues and, in a bottom-up fashion, is giving hopes that governance can change, if all water actors start taking responsibility. Through social media, education, and artistic initiatives, as well as actions on the ground by NGOs in the rural and the urban environment, people can start understanding better what the issues at stake really are and start suggesting solutions that work for them and even initiate some. Within this context, the Berber movement, because of its entirely interdisciplinary approach of water management practices, definitely has something to say at all levels – technological, economic, social, political, and of course cultural. It constitutes the living memory of a rich and inspiring water heritage and, more than ever in the history of Morocco, should learn how to express itself and should be listened to.

Examples of economies that rely on intensive, industrial, monocultural cash crops abound around the world. Examples of Western economies that encourage imports of such crops – hence virtual water – therefore too. Whilst climate change debates mostly focus on problems induced by industrial activities that are high emitters of greenhouse gases, it is also time to systemically examine how water resources, as a sign of CC effects, need to be better understood and managed. Water resources are not just natural resources to be used in economic activities. It is at the core of democratic ecological economic development.

Index

For Product Safety Concerns and Information please contact our EU
representative GPSR@taylorandfrancis.com
Taylor & Francis Verlag GmbH, Kaufingerstraße 24, 80331 München, Germany